COTSWOLD
CLASSIC WALKS

WRITTEN AND PHOTOGRAPHED BY WILLIAM FRICKER

LOCATOR MAP

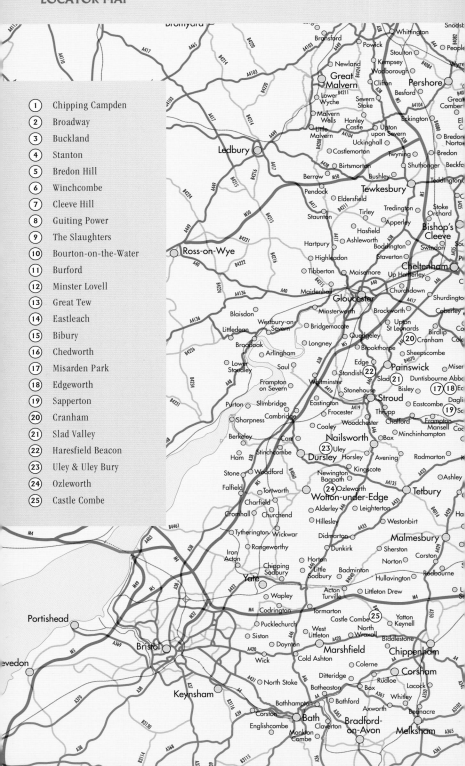

To my Cotswold Walking Companions: Caroline, Isabella, Harry, Flora and Alice.

Research & Text by William Fricker. Photography by William Fricker (unless credited with an initial ss - supplied by subject).

First published in the United Kingdom, in 2010, by Goldeneye, Braunton, Devon EX33 1HW, Second Edition, 2014.

Text copyright © 2014, William Fricker. Photographs copyright © 2014 William Fricker.

Maps supplied by Goldeneye's Digital Database. Maps copyright © Goldeneye, 2014.

Cartography by Cox Cartographic Ltd & PC Graphics Ltd. Original Design and layout by Chris Dyer. Second Edition amends by Camouka

Correct Information. The contents of this publication were believed to be correct and accurate at the time of printing. However, Goldeneye accepts no responsibility for any errors, omissions or changes in the details given, or for the consequences arising thereto, from the use of this book. However, the publishers would greatly appreciate your time in notifying us of any changes or new attractions (or places to eat, drink and stay) that you consider merit inclusion in the next edition. Your comments are most welcome for we value the views, suggestions and feedback of our readers.

Stanway

The Cotswolds epitomise the romantic notion of the traditional English scene: picture-postcard images of rolling green hills overlooking villages of golden stone cottages, manor houses and majestic churches. This image is no dream but is clearly evident when you walk the routes described in this book. And, no better way to experience the setting of this dramatic architecture than to walk from village to village, or along the western escarpment that affords spectacular views across the Severn Vale and towards the Welsh hills. But, first you must explore and savour the village from whence your walk begins and stroll through this rolling landscape of sheep pastures, trout streams and dry-stone walls.

The Cotswold landscape was formed by geological upheaval and by the interference of Man; i.e. by the limestone and wool. The Cotswold hills are the highest part of a band of oolitic limestone which tilts in a south east direction running from near the Dorset coast to south Lincolnshire. From the steep escarpments in the west, the Cotswold hills gently descend in an easterly direction, bisected by fast-flowing trout streams feeding the River Thames.

This limestone is a superb building material and is malleable and easily cut into beautiful shapes, it weathers extreme climate and looks attractive in all light. The wool merchants of the Middle Ages developed the fleece and laid the foundations of prosperity and it was these merchants who built the great 'Wool' churches, manor houses and tithe barns so splendidly evident in Broadway, Burford, Chipping Campden and Winchcombe.

These walks are categorised as easy, moderate or strenuous. A modicum of fitness is required. Waterproof footwear is advised and a light rucksack with cagoule, refreshments and spare jumper will not go amiss. The topography is of an undulating landscape and to link various routes we have used the Cotswold Way which can be hard-going in places and can resemble the South West coastal footpath as an energy sapping device. A number of the routes do join up and can make an interesting figure-of-eight for those looking for an all-day walk.

Our mapping has been tried and tested these past twelve years and you don't need to be an experienced map-reader to follow these routes. The maps illustrate regular points of reference to make you feel secure: water troughs, stiles, a special tree. And, you should also be able to follow the routes just by reading the boxes of text. Of course, landmarks do disappear and stiles or gates move from time to time so please let me know if you encounter any such changes.

I have also included a few suggestions for accommodation and eating/drinking venues. This list is by no means exhaustive but I have tried to provide venues that are used to walkers and also children and dogs. During the final stages of putting this book to bed; gathering last-minute photographs and re-checking the routes I dropped my motor-cycle on my foot, cracking it which severely restricted my movements for three months. It occurred to me that walking was a privilege that I had always taken for granted. Indeed, these sentiments have deepened by the day as I note the endless stream of young men returning from Afghanistan with appalling injuries. So be with good cheer and a hearty breakfast inside you, go forth and take advantage of these English hills while you can.

Happy Walking,

William Fricker

WHICH WALK TO UNDERTAKE

With 25 circular walks, this book will help you find a base to escape from your car and enjoy a weekend of fresh air and exercise. Some walks offer various route options or links to other walks. How to decide which walk to undertake? Which walks are best for kids, dogs or pub lunches? Where are the best views? Where to find solitude? We have made some suggestions to help guide you in your choice. These are by no means the only options in this book but might help you get started.

1. Pushchairs

Misarden Park walk. At just 1.5miles and with only about 20 metres of rough track and one stile, this walk is suitable for pushchairs. Furthermore, the surroundings are beautiful, ranging from woodland to lakes with abundant wildlife – plenty of interest for both parents and kids.

2. Families

The Eastleach-Leach Valley walk provides plenty of interest to all ages. If 4.5 miles is too long for smaller children, there is a handy shortcut. Alternatively, Guiting Power is a mostly flat, wooded walk of 3 miles with plenty of flora and fauna.

3. Dogs

Cleave Common is popular with dog walkers as dogs can run free. With only a few stiles once you leave Cleave Common and great views for the humans, this is by far the best dog walk in this book. Note of caution: if you prefer to walk your dog away from the madding crowd, Haresfield Beacon or Sapperton are good alternative walks.

4. Pubs

If you like to get the hard work out of the way and finish your walk with a well-earned rest at a local pub, the Sapperton walk provides you with a delightful watering hole in the Bell Inn. If you need something to spur you on to the halfway point, the Cranham walk provides a rest stop in the Butcher's Arms, Sheepscombe as well as a good walkers' pit stop a little further on at the Foston's Ash Inn.

5. Views

For a variety of views from far reaching landscapes to views overlooking quaint Cotswold villages, the Painswick-Slad Valley walk provides beautiful English landscapes in all directions. For more dramatic tastes, the views from Broadway Tower take in 13 counties or there are fine views towards the River Severn and Welsh Hills from Uley Bury Hillfort.

Misarden Park

Eastleach

Cleeve Hill

The Bell at Sapperton

6. Weekends Away

If you want to avoid using the car, there are plenty of towns to make your base for a weekend away with great eating places and a choice of places to stay. Based in Broadway, you could undertake the Broadway-Broadway Tower walk and the Buckland-Laverton walk. Chipping Campden and Painswick also provide a choice of walks.

7. Public Transport

If you base yourself in Painswick which has bus links to Stroud railway station, you will have a choice of two walks on your doorstep. The Painswick-Slad Valley walk which starts in the town and the Haresfield Beacon walk which is connected to Painswick by a short link route.

8. Woodland

Cranham-Sheepscombe walk. Plenty of interest including Saltridge Wood Nature Reserve. The route is mainly through or along the edge of woodland which is particularly beautiful in early summer and autumn.

9. Bluebells and Springtime

The descent from Broadway Tower passes through a wood carpeted in wild flowers and abundant with bluebells in spring. Delightful after the open vistas from Broadway Tower.

10. Peace and Quiet

For wild, beautiful and remote landscapes, the deep combes of Ozleworth Bottom are for you. The isolated landscape teems with wildlife and flowers.

Slad Valley

Laverton Hill

Haresfield Beacon

Saltridge Wood

Broadway Tower

Ozleworth Church

Parish Church of St James

The route picks up the start of the Cotswold Way in Chipping Campden and follows it up to Dover's Hill, scene of the Cotswold Olympick Games. It then follows the edge of the Scarp to provide splendid views over the Vale of Evesham, before climbing up through enchanting woodland and then descending back into Chipping Campden.

Distance
4.25 miles/6.8km

Minimum Time
3 hours

Grade/Level of Difficulty
Easy/Moderate

Terrain/Paths
Tarmac, stone tracks, woodland paths.

Landscape
Arable fields, woodland and sheep pastures.

Dogs
Keep under control - beware livestock. Short section along road has grass verges.

Public Toilets
Chipping Campden High Street

Parking (P)
Beside Market Hall or at Dover's Hill P.

Recommended Start/Finish
Market Hall, Chipping Campden or Dover's Hill.

Location
On the B4081, off the A44 Broadway to Moreton in Marsh road.

Link to other walks in this Guide
Broadway Walk via Fish Hill.

Features of Interest...

Almshouses. You will pass these on your left as you make your way toward the Parish Church. Built about the same time as the Market Hall (in 1627) by the town's wealthy benefactor, Sir Baptist Hicks.

Chipping Campden. The Jewel of the Cotswolds, indeed the architectural gem of this region with a superb harmony of honey-coloured stone houses. A major wool centre in the Middle Ages between the C14 and C17s. The village's prosperity is mirrored by the handsome buildings such as St James' Church, the Lodges at Campden House, Almshouses, Grevel's House, the Woolstaplers Hall and Market Hall. If you choose to visit just one Cotswold village, make sure it's this one. There is no better introduction.

Court Barn Museum. Set opposite the Almshouses, a celebration of the town's association with the "Arts & Crafts Movement". An exhibition of silver, jewellery, ceramics, Sculpture, industrial design and more, all beautifully laid out by the Guild of Handicraft Trust. Open Tu-Sa 10-5 & BH Ms (- 4 Oct-Mar). www.courtbarn.org.uk

Dover's Hill. A natural amphitheatre on a spur of the Cotswolds with magnificent views over the Vale of Evesham. The 'Olympick Games & Scuttlebrook Wake' have been held here since 1612, and take place the Friday and Saturday following Spring Bank Holiday.

Grevel's House. William Grevel, one of the wealthiest wool merchants, is remembered in the church on a brass transcription which reads: 'the flower of the wool merchants of all England'. Built by him, the house has exquisitely decorated windows, gargoyles and sundial.

Hart Silversmiths, The Old Silk Mill. Founded in 1888 as part of the 'Arts & Crafts' movement. The Harts gold and silversmith workshop is the last operating remnant of the Guild of Handicraft which C R Ashbee established in 1888, And which moved to this village in 1902. Café. Open all year 01386 841100 www.hartsilversmiths.co.uk

Market Hall. This iconic image of Chipping Campden was funded by Sir Baptist Hicks (merchant banker) in 1627 for the cheese and butter markets. It is Jacobean.

St James' Church. Famous 'Wool' church of Norman origins but restored in the C15. Perpendicular nave, elegant tower, C15 cope, and a unique pair of C15 altar hangings. Superb brasses of the Woolstaplers. C15 falcon lecturn. Open daily.

Where to Eat, Drink & Stay...

Badgers Hall. Charming C15 house with mullioned windows and exposed beams housing a B&B and tearoom. Light lunches or substantial afternoon cream teas available to visitors and guests. No pets or young children. 01386 840839 www.badgershall.co.uk

Bantam Tea Rooms. C17 building situated opposite the old Market Hall. Afternoon teas available inside or in the tea garden. B&B with private guest lounge and off street parking. 01386 840386 www.bantamtea-rooms.co.uk

Campden Pantry. Coffee shop and delicatessen offering drinks and light meals with a friendly Cotswold flavour. Takeway meals, too. 01386 841861

Cotswold House Hotel, The Square. Boutique hotel in the centre of Chipping Campden. Contemporary restaurant and Hicks Brasserie for more informal dining. 01386 840330 www.cotswoldhouse.com

Eight Bells Inn, Church Street. C14 inn full of rustic charm contrasts well with modern cuisine and bright bedrooms. Fresh fare. B&B. 01386 840371 www.eightbellsinn.co.uk

Kings Hotel, The Square. 14 stylish bedrooms. Large gardens for al fresco eating and drinking. Brasserie and bar offering lighter meals and local beers. Pre-walk breakfasts recommended (booking essential). 01386 840256 www.kingscampden.co.uk

Michaels Mediterranean Restaurant. Greek and modern Mediterranean cuisine, served in a relaxed setting. Open for coffee, lunches, takeaways and evening meals. 01386 840826 www.michaelsmediterranean.co.uk

Seymour House B&B. Large family home, and one of the village's iconic houses furnished for your every comfort, and conveniently located on the High Street. 01386 840064 www.seymurhousebandb.co.uk

Thatched Cottage in Westington

Cotswold Way, Long Hill

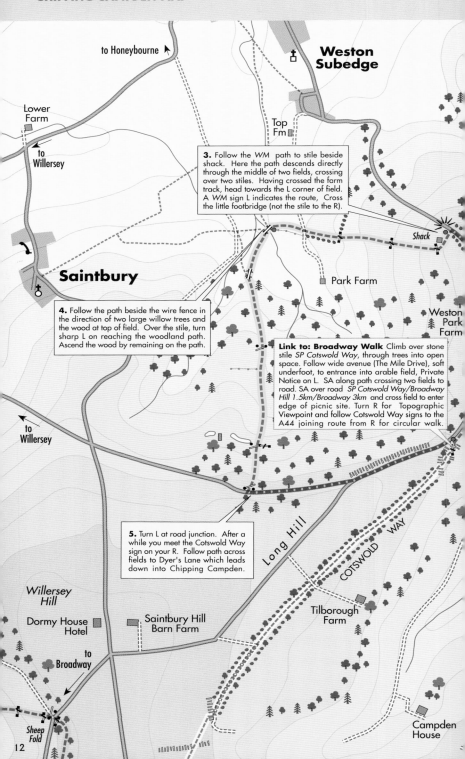

to Honeybourne

Weston Subedge

Lower Farm

to Willersey

Top Fm

3. Follow the *WM* path to stile beside shack. Here the path descends directly through the middle of two fields, crossing over two stiles. Having crossed the farm track, head towards the L corner of field. A *WM* sign L indicates the route, Cross the little footbridge (not the stile to the R).

Shack

Saintbury

Park Farm

Weston Park Farm

4. Follow the path beside the wire fence in the direction of two large willow trees and the wood at top of field. Over the stile, turn sharp L on reaching the woodland path. Ascend the wood by remaining on the path.

Link to: Broadway Walk Climb over stone stile *SP Cotswold Way*, through trees into open space. Follow wide avenue (The Mile Drive), soft underfoot, to entrance into arable field, Private Notice on L. SA along path crossing two fields to road. SA over road *SP Cotswold Way/Broadway Hill 1.5km/Broadway 3km* and cross field to enter edge of picnic site. Turn R for Topographic Viewpoint and follow Cotswold Way signs to the A44 joining route from R for circular walk.

to Willersey

5. Turn L at road junction. After a while you meet the Cotswold Way sign on your R. Follow path across fields to Dyer's Lane which leads down into Chipping Campden.

Long Hill

COTSWOLD WAY

Willersey Hill

Dormy House Hotel

Saintbury Hill Barn Farm

Tilborough Farm

to Broadway

Campden House

Sheep Fold

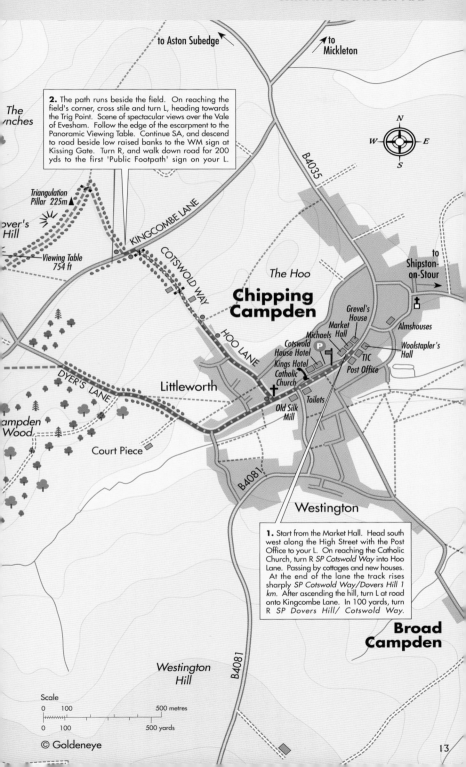

2. The path runs beside the field. On reaching the field's corner, cross stile and turn L, heading towards the Trig Point. Scene of spectacular views over the Vale of Evesham. Follow the edge of the escarpment to the Panoramic Viewing Table. Continue SA, and descend to road beside low raised banks to the WM sign at Kissing Gate. Turn R, and walk down road for 200 yds to the first 'Public Footpath' sign on your L.

to Aston Subedge

to Mickleton

The nches

The Hoo

B4035

Triangulation Pillar 225m ▲

over's Hill

Viewing Table 754 ft

KINGCOMBE LANE

COTSWOLD WAY

Chipping Campden

Grevel's House

Market Hall

Michaels

Almshouses

to Shipston-on-Stour

HOO LANE

Cotswold House Hotel

Kings Hotel

Catholic Church

P

Woolstapler's Hall

TIC

Post Office

DYER'S LANE

Littleworth

ampden Wood

Court Piece

Toilets

Old Silk Mill

B4081

Westington

1. Start from the Market Hall. Head south west along the High Street with the Post Office to your L. On reaching the Catholic Church, turn R *SP Cotswold Way* into Hoo Lane. Passing by cottages and new houses. At the end of the lane the track rises sharply *SP Cotswold Way/Dovers Hill 1 km*. After ascending the hill, turn L at road onto Kingcombe Lane. In 100 yards, turn R *SP Dovers Hill/ Cotswold Way*.

Broad Campden

Westington Hill

B4081

Scale

0   100   500 metres

0   100   500 yards

© Goldeneye

Broadway Tower

Broadway epitomises English domestic architecture at its finest, and so it is worth spending some time here before you venture forth out of the village up a relatively steep climb followed by a woodland walk and superb views over the vale. From Broadway Tower, it is possible, on a clear day, to see 13 counties. The descent is through a wood carpeted in wild flowers (bluebells in spring).

Distance
4.5 miles/7.2km

Minimum Time
3 hours

Grade/Level of Difficulty
Easy/Moderate

Terrain/Paths
Grass, farm tracks, paths.

Landscape
Rolling countryside, woodland.

Dogs
Fairly good for dogs - can run free in woodland. Keep under control around livestock.

Public Toilets
Broadway P & Broadway Tower Country Park.

Parking (P)
Broadway - behind High Street. There are two car parks in the village.

Recommended Start/Finish
Broadway P

Location
Broadway lies off the A44 midway between Evesham and Stow on the Wold, or on the B4632 midway between Cheltenham and Stratford upon Avon.

Link to other walks
35 minute link from Fish Hill to join Chipping Campden walk. 40 minute link to Buckland, return via Cotswold Way and Lydbrook.

Features of Interest...

Broadway. 'The Painted Lady of the Cotswolds' is a term often used to describe this beautiful village. The honey-coloured stone captivates the visitor today as it did in the C19 when William Morris and his pre-Raphaelite friends settled here. A slow walk up the High Street will reveal some large and impressive houses that have been homes to Edward Elgar, JM Barrie (Peter Pan), Ralph Vaughan Williams, Sir Gerald Navarro MP and Laura Ashley. These great houses with bow windows, dormers & finely graduated stone roofs are usually hidden behind statuesque gates. There are a number of fine hotels, restaurants, tearooms, art galleries and a splendid bookshop.

Broadway Tower Country Park. A unique Cotswold attraction: an C18 folly tower with historical and geographical exhibitions. Formerly one of the country retreats of the pre-Raphaelite, William Morris. Red deer are bred here, and there are nature walks, as well as an adventure playground, barbecue areas and a classy café/restaurant with gift shop. Superb views from the Tower - a clear day provides a view of 13 counties. Open daily, all year 10-5. 01386 852390 www.broadwaytower.co.uk

Fish Hill Woods. Attractive woodland providing superb views.

Gordon Russell Design Museum. Displays the work of the renowned C20 furniture designer who started in 1920. Open daily from 11, all year except Ms & closed in January. www.gordonrussellmuseum.org

St Eadburgh's Church. A rare architectural gem of almost perfect proportions with a mix of C12-C18 additions. Superb brass work, topiary in churchyard, interesting tombstones and a welcome retreat from the hustle and bustle of Broadway.

Where to Eat & Drink...

Broadway Deli, 29 High Street. For those who are self-catering, treat yourself to a trip to this excellent deli with a passion for organic and ethically produced food. Great for picnics, late breakfasts and delish snacks to sustain you on your walk. 01386 853040 www.broadwaydeli.co.uk

Crown & Trumpet Inn, Church Street. A necessary pit stop as you enter Broadway from the Cotswold Way. Music Sa evenings. Monthly jazz and blues nights. B&B. 01386 853202

Market Pantry, 31 High Street. A cute, little café ideal for a late breakfast prior to walking the Cotswold Way. 01386 858318 www.marketpantry.co.uk

Prego Broadway, 32 High Street. Primi or Pizza, and a menu for Vegetarians, too. A quiet corner of Italian style to assuage your hunger for antipasti, and a glass of Chianti. Open daily. 01386 306670

Russells Fish & Chips. You can't get away from the fact that this staple diet has kept families in clover for years. It's a pretty little restaurant, too, and a wee bit classy. Open daily. www.russellsfishandchips.co.uk

The Horse and the Hounds, 54 High Street. Ideal stop off point for a drink at the end of a day walking. Dog friendly. B&B. 01386 852287 www.horse-and-hound.co.uk

Tisanes, 21 The Green. A friendly tea room set in a C17 Cotswold stone building full of charm and overlooking the Village Green. Garden. Homemade cakes. 01386 853296   www.tisanes-tearooms.co.uk

Where to Stay...

Luggers Hall, Springfield Lane. Built by the Victorian Royal Academy artist Alfred Parsons, this listed building is set in two acres of landscaped gardens. Peaceful and tranquil setting, yet less than two minutes walk from Broadway's village centre. B&B. Also, Dove cottage – self catering two bedroom period cottage on Upper High Street available for holiday lets. 01386 852040 www.luggershall.com

Mill Hay House, Snowshill Road. Imposing Queen Anne house provides luxurious B&B on the outskirts of Broadway. No children U-12. No dogs. 01386 852498 www.millhay.co.uk

Olive Branch Guest House, 78 High Street. A B&B of long standing, and one that has traded for 50 years. It is convenient, comfortable and often doing great deals for 2/3 day breaks. 01386 853440 www.theolivebranch-broadway.com

Russell's, 20 High Street. A great place to eat in the North Cotswolds, whether it be lunch, or dinner. So, feast on their food, then settle into one of their contemporary, comfortable bedrooms with all the latest mod cons. 01386 853555   www.russellsofbroadway.co.uk

Russell's ss

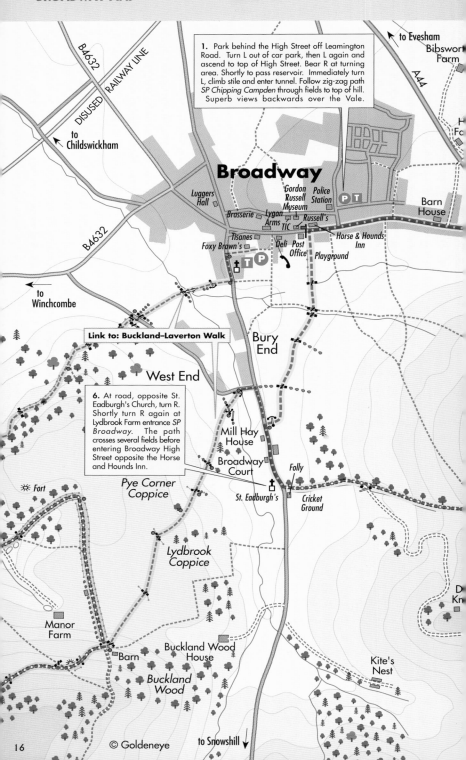

1. Park behind the High Street off Leamington Road. Turn L out of car park, then L again and ascend to top of High Street. Bear R at turning area. Shortly to pass reservoir. Immediately turn L, climb stile and enter tunnel. Follow zig-zag path *SP Chipping Campden* through fields to top of hill. Superb views backwards over the Vale.

to Evesham

Bibsworth Farm

A44

Broadway

Luggers Hall

Gordon Russell Museum

Police Station

P T

Barn House

Brasserie

Lygan Arms

Russell's

TIC

Tisanes

Foxy Brown's

Deli

Post Office

Horse & Hounds Inn

Playground

T P

B4632

DISUSED RAILWAY LINE

B4632

to Childswickham

to Winchcombe

Link to: Buckland–Laverton Walk

Bury End

West End

6. At road, opposite St. Eadburgh's Church, turn R. Shortly turn R again at Lydbrook Farm entrance *SP Broadway*. The path crosses several fields before entering Broadway High Street opposite the Horse and Hounds Inn.

Mill Hay House

Broadway Court

Folly

St. Eadburgh's

Cricket Ground

☀ Fort

Pye Corner Coppice

Lydbrook Coppice

Manor Farm

Barn

Buckland Wood House

Buckland Wood

Kite's Nest

D Kn

to Snowshill ↓

© Goldeneye

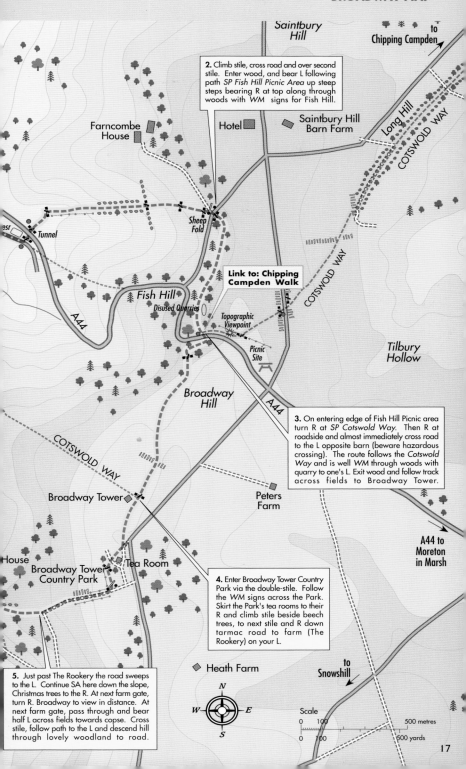

Saintbury Hill

to Chipping Campden

2. Climb stile, cross road and over second stile. Enter wood, and bear L following path *SP Fish Hill Picnic Area* up steep steps bearing R at top along through woods with *WM* signs for Fish Hill.

Long Hill

COTSWOLD WAY

Farncombe House

Hotel

Saintbury Hill Barn Farm

Sheep Fold

Tunnel

COTSWOLD WAY

Link to: Chipping Campden Walk

Fish Hill

Disused Quarries

Topographic Viewpoint

Picnic Site

Tilbury Hollow

A44

Broadway Hill

A44

3. On entering edge of Fish Hill Picnic area turn R at *SP Cotswold Way*. Then R at roadside and almost immediately cross road to the L opposite barn (beware hazardous crossing). The route follows the *Cotswold Way* and is well *WM* through woods with quarry to one's L. Exit wood and follow track across fields to Broadway Tower.

COTSWOLD WAY

Broadway Tower

Peters Farm

A44 to Moreton in Marsh

House

Broadway Tower Country Park

Tea Room

4. Enter Broadway Tower Country Park via the double-stile. Follow the *WM* signs across the Park. Skirt the Park's tea rooms to their R and climb stile beside beech trees, to next stile and R down tarmac road to farm (The Rookery) on your L.

Heath Farm

to Snowshill

5. Just past The Rookery the road sweeps to the L. Continue SA here down the slope, Christmas trees to the R. At next farm gate, turn R. Broadway to view in distance. At next farm gate, pass through and bear half L across fields towards copse. Cross stile, follow path to the L and descend hill through lovely woodland to road.

N
W — E
S

Scale
0   100   500 metres
0   100   500 yards

Ascending Laverton Hill

Buckland to Laverton is a short walk connecting two quiet villages via a steep climb up to and along, the Cotswold Way. The views make up for the steep climb and the descent to Laverton is easy-going. Broadway to Buckland is easy-going across fields and through pretty woodland. Climbing steeply up to the Cotswold Way with a gentle descent providing fine views to Broadway.

Distance
2.75 miles/4.4km.

Minimum Time
1.5 hours

Grade/Level of Difficulty
Easy/Moderate

Terrain/Paths
Farm track, rough path, grass.

Landscape
Undulating escarpment, sheep pastures.

Dogs
Lots of farm fields so dogs to be kept under control throughout. Beware livestock.

Public Toilets
Broadway

Parking (P)
Beside church

Recommended Start/Finish
Buckland Church

Location
Buckland is 2 miles south of Broadway, just off the B4632.

Link to other walks in this Guide
Stanton to Stanway Walk. Circular route from edge of Laverton to Stanton via Cotswold Way and Shenberrow Farm.

Features of Interest...

Buckland. A tranquil, linear village where time appears to have stood still. Noted for its Country House Hotel, stone cottages, stables, nursery and holiday cottage complex.

Buckland Rectory. The oldest and most complete rectory in the county. Notable Great Hall with timbered roof. Open occasionally for village events.

St Michael's Church, Buckland. An exquisite church preserved with an almost undisturbed history from the C13 to the C17. Beautiful roof, painted and wood panelled. C14 tower with gargoyles. C15 stained glass in East window restored by William Morris. Not to be missed, the wainscotting: medieval wooden benches along the far wall as you enter, the Hazel Bowl made in 1607 of Dutch maple with a silver rim, the Buckland Pall and C15 embroidered vestments from the V&A Museum, London. Sadly, the medieval frescoes were removed by the restorer FS Waller in 1885.

Where to Stay...

Buckland Manor Hotel. The benchmark for the Country House Hotel, so if you seek quiet, understated luxury, and a haven of relaxation, none better (at a price). Formal dress code for dinner - the exquisite cuisine deserves your respect. Open all year. Non-residents welcome for cream teas. 01386 852626
www.bucklandmanor.co.uk

Burhill Farm, Buckland.
Peaceful setting. Two en-suite bedrooms. B&B.
01386 858171 www.burhillfarm.co.uk

Nearby Broadway has a wealth of tea rooms and inns for alternative dining and accommodation options.

Buckland Manor Hotel ss

Sheep Pasture, Laverton

St Mary's Church, Buckland

Cotswold Way, Buckland Wood

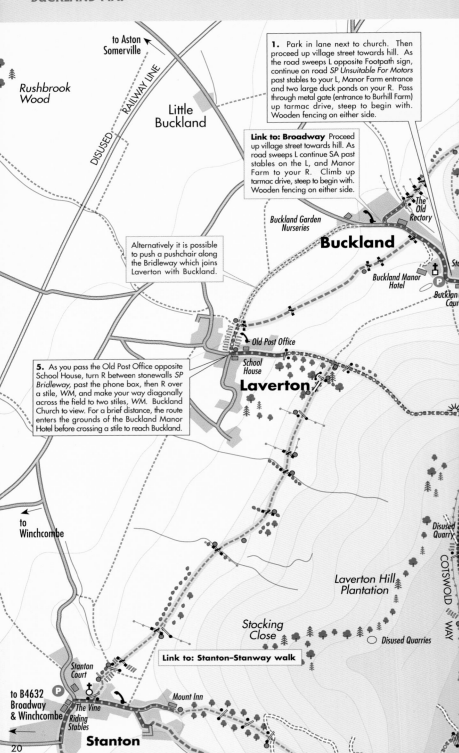

to Aston
Somerville

*Rushbrook
Wood*

Little
Buckland

RAILWAY LINE

DISUSED

1. Park in lane next to church. Then proceed up village street towards hill. As the road sweeps L opposite Footpath sign, continue on road *SP Unsuitable For Motors* past stables to your L, Manor Farm entrance and two large duck ponds on your R. Pass through metal gate (entrance to Burhill Farm) up tarmac drive, steep to begin with. Wooden fencing on either side.

Link to: Broadway Proceed up village street towards hill. As road sweeps L continue SA past stables on the L, and Manor Farm to your R. Climb up tarmac drive, steep to begin with. Wooden fencing on either side.

Buckland Garden
Nurseries

Buckland

*The Old
Rectory*

Sta

Alternatively it is possible to push a pushchair along the Bridleway which joins Laverton with Buckland.

*Buckland Manor
Hotel*

Buckland
Cour

Old Post Office

5. As you pass the Old Post Office opposite School House, turn R between stonewalls *SP Bridleway*, past the phone box, then R over a stile, *WM*, and make your way diagonally across the field to two stiles, *WM*. Buckland Church to view. For a brief distance, the route enters the grounds of the Buckland Manor Hotel before crossing a stile to reach Buckland.

*School
House*

Laverton

to
Winchcombe

*Disused
Quarry*

COTSWOLD WAY

*Laverton Hill
Plantation*

*Stocking
Close*

Disused Quarries

Link to: Stanton–Stanway walk

*Stanton
Court*

to B4632
Broadway
& Winchcombe

The Vine

Mount Inn

*Riding
Stables*

Stanton

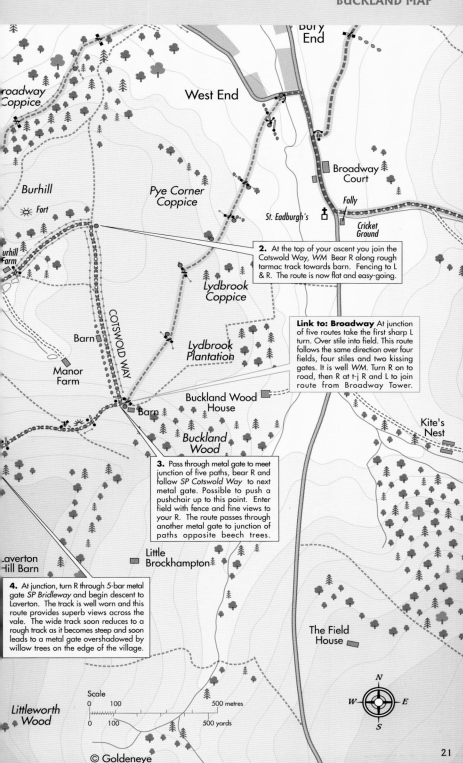

West End

Bury End

Broadway Coppice

Broadway Court

Burhill

Fort

Pye Corner Coppice

Folly

St. Eadburgh's

Cricket Ground

2. At the top of your ascent you join the Cotswold Way, *WM* Bear R along rough tarmac track towards barn. Fencing to L & R. The route is now flat and easy-going.

Burhill Farm

Lydbrook Coppice

COTSWOLD WAY

Barn

Lydbrook Plantation

Link to: Broadway At junction of five routes take the first sharp L turn. Over stile into field. This route follows the same direction over four fields, four stiles and two kissing gates. It is well *WM*. Turn R on to road, then R at t-j R and L to join route from Broadway Tower.

Manor Farm

Barn

Buckland Wood House

Kite's Nest

Buckland Wood

3. Pass through metal gate to meet junction of five paths, bear R and follow *SP Cotswold Way* to next metal gate. Possible to push a pushchair up to this point. Enter field with fence and fine views to your R. The route passes through another metal gate to junction of paths opposite beech trees.

Laverton Hill Barn

Little Brockhampton

4. At junction, turn R through 5-bar metal gate *SP Bridleway* and begin descent to Laverton. The track is well worn and this route provides superb views across the vale. The wide track soon reduces to a rough track as it becomes steep and soon leads to a metal gate overshadowed by willow trees on the edge of the village.

The Field House

Littleworth Wood

Scale

0   100   500 metres

0   100   500 yards

N
W   E
S

© Goldeneye

Stanway House & Churchyard

The Stanton to Stanway route at first follows the Cotswold Way with a steady climb up to Shenberrow Hill. Thereafter the route descends through pretty woodland passing by Estate workers' cottages and an orchard, then from Stanway through beautiful parkland and arable fields. The Stanton to Laverton route travels north through open fields to join the Buckland to Laverton walk returning via the Cotswold Way and Shenberrow Hill with a link to Snowshill at Shenberrow.

Distance
Walk 1: 4.5 miles/7.2 km. Walk 2: 3 miles.

Minimum Time
Walk 1: 3 hours. Walk 2: 2 hours.

Grade/Level of Difficulty
Moderate

Terrain/Paths
Stone paths, woodland, grassy turf.

Landscape
Rolling escarpment, woodland, domestic architecture.

Dogs
Large section of woodland where dogs can run free. Keep under control around livestock. Popular with local dog walkers.

Public Toilets
None

Parking (P)
Stanton P

Recommended Start/Finish
Stanton P, or Stanway.

Location
Situated between Winchcombe and Broadway just off the B4632.

Link to other walks in this Guide
Buckland to Laverton & Snowshill Walks

Features of Interest...

Shenberrow Hill fort. Iron Age settlement inhabited around 2,000 BC. Superb viewpoint at 280 ft.

Snowshill. This charming and unspoilt hilltop village is a short distance by car from Broadway. There's a striking church, a pub and a row of much photographed cottages opposite Snowshill Manor.

Snowshill Manor (NT). A Cotswold manor house containing Charles Paget Wade's extraordinary collection of craftsmanship and design amounting to some 22,000 items from toys to musical instruments, Samurai armour to clocks and bicycles. Open W-Su mid-Mar to 1 Nov 12-5, grounds, restaurant and shop from 11. 01386 852410
www.nationaltrust.org.uk

Stanton. Charming village with houses of warm honey-coloured stone. Restored by Sir Philip Scott, 1903-37. Centre for equine excellence in the Vine, a popular horse riding centre.

Stanway. Estate village owned by the Earl of Wemyss and March and dominated by Stanway House in the grounds of which stand one of the country's finest tithe barns. The C17 gatehouse is exceptional, and behind the church, across the road is the thatched cricket pavilion set on staddle stones. The little Church of St Peter has C14 origins.

Stanway House & Water Garden. This exquisite Jacobean Manor House and Gatehouse is built from the local stone known as Guiting Yellow which lights up when the sun touches it. All is set within an enchanting and ancient park designed by a numerologist. The partially restored C18 Cascade and Canal was designed by the highly respected Charles Bridgman, and is now open June to Aug, Tu & Th 2-5. Dogs on lead. 01386 584469
www.stanwayfountain.co.uk

St Michael's Church, Stanton. Impressive Perpendicular tower. Much is C12 -15 with wall paintings, Jacobean pulpit, but its fame was associated with the many visits of John Wesley, the Methodist preacher.

Where to Eat and Drink...

Mount Inn, Stanton. Situated on a rise at the edge of Stanton the Inn's unique position provides the most spectacular panoramic views across the Vale of Evesham towards the Malvern Hills & even the Black Welsh mountains beyond. On a summer's evening it is the most perfect spot to watch the sunset & enjoy a pint of Donnington Brewery's traditional ale. Used to walkers and their dogs, the Inn serves a range of excellent food to suit all levels of hunger. Now considered to be one of the Cotswold's culinary high spots. 01386 584316
www.themountinn.co.uk

Snowshill Arms, Snowshill.
Traditional Cotswold pub with large garden. Good range of food. Children welcome. 01386 852653

Where to Stay...

The Vine, Stanton. B&B designed for horse lovers. Riding lessons for all levels available. The owner's popular pub rides include an hour's lunch stop at a traditional pub. 01386 584250
www.cotswoldsriding.co.uk

Stanton

Snowshill Manor

Stanway Park

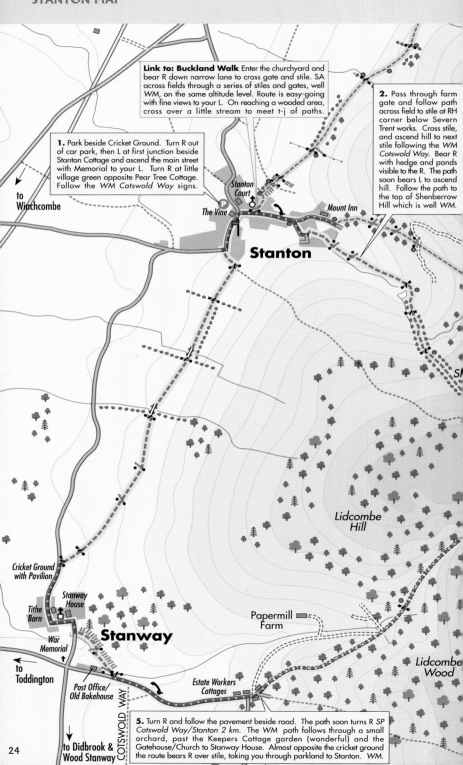

Link to: Buckland Walk Enter the churchyard and bear R down narrow lane to cross gate and stile. SA across fields through a series of stiles and gates, well *WM*, on the same altitude level. Route is easy-going with fine views to your L. On reaching a wooded area, cross over a little stream to meet t-j of paths.

2. Pass through farm gate and follow path across field to stile at RH corner below Severn Trent works. Cross stile, and ascend hill to next stile following the *WM Cotswold Way*. Bear R with hedge and ponds visible to the R. The path soon bears L to ascend hill. Follow the path to the top of Shenberrow Hill which is well *WM*.

1. Park beside Cricket Ground. Turn R out of car park, then L at first junction beside Stanton Cottage and ascend the main street with Memorial to your L. Turn R at little village green opposite Pear Tree Cottage. Follow the *WM Cotswold Way* signs.

to Winchcombe

Stanton Court

The Vine

Mount Inn

Stanton

Lidcombe Hill

Cricket Ground with Pavilion

Stanway House

Tithe Barn

Stanway

War Memorial

to Toddington

Papermill Farm

Lidcombe Wood

Post Office/ Old Bakehouse

COTSWOLD WAY

Estate Workers Cottages

to Didbrook & Wood Stanway

5. Turn R and follow the pavement beside road. The path soon turns R *SP Cotswold Way/Stanton 2 km*. The *WM* path follows through a small orchard, past the Keepers Cottage garden (wonderful) and the Gatehouse/Church to Stanway House. Almost opposite the cricket ground the route bears R over stile, taking you through parkland to Stanton. *WM*.

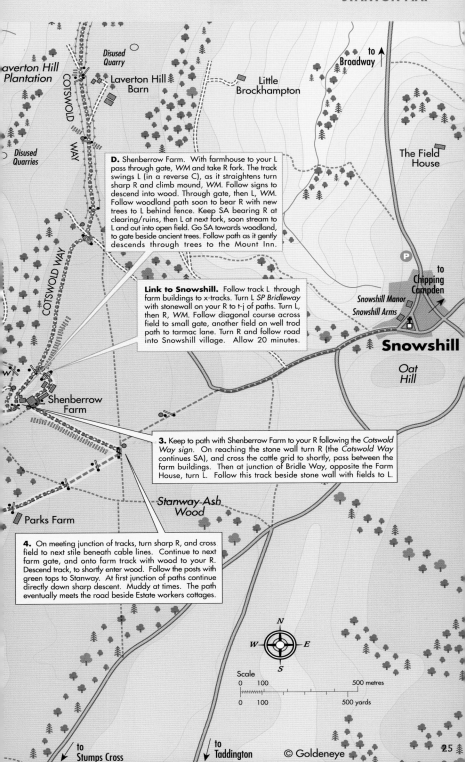

to Broadway

Laverton Hill Plantation

Disused Quarry

COTSWOLD WAY

Laverton Hill Barn

Little Brockhampton

Disused Quarries

The Field House

D. Shenberrow Farm. With farmhouse to your L pass through gate, *WM* and take R fork. The track swings L (in a reverse C), as it straightens turn sharp R and climb mound, *WM*. Follow signs to descend into wood. Through gate, then L, *WM*. Follow woodland path soon to bear R with new trees to L behind fence. Keep SA bearing R at clearing/ruins, then L at next fork, soon stream to L and out into open field. Go SA towards woodland, to gate beside ancient trees. Follow path as it gently descends through trees to the Mount Inn.

COTSWOLD WAY

Link to Snowshill. Follow track L through farm buildings to x-tracks. Turn L *SP Bridleway* with stonewall on your R to t-j of paths. Turn L, then R, *WM*. Follow diagonal course across field to small gate, another field on well trod path to tarmac lane. Turn R and follow road into Snowshill village. Allow 20 minutes.

Snowshill Manor

Snowshill Arms

to Chipping Campden

Snowshill

Oat Hill

W

Shenberrow Farm

3. Keep to path with Shenberrow Farm to your R following the *Cotswold Way sign*. On reaching the stone wall turn R (the *Cotswold Way* continues SA), and cross the cattle grid to shortly, pass between the farm buildings. Then at junction of Bridle Way, opposite the Farm House, turn L. Follow this track beside stone wall with fields to L.

Stanway Ash Wood

Parks Farm

4. On meeting junction of tracks, turn sharp R, and cross field to next stile beneath cable lines. Continue to next farm gate, and onto farm track with wood to your R. Descend track, to shortly enter wood. Follow the posts with green tops to Stanway. At first junction of paths continue directly down sharp descent. Muddy at times. The path eventually meets the road beside Estate workers cottages.

N
W   E
S

Scale
0   100   500 metres
0   100   500 yards

to Stumps Cross

to Taddington

© Goldeneye

Wychavon Way, Fiddler's Knap

A circumnavigation of Bredon Hill is a fine introduction to the beautiful villages of Kemerton, Overbury, Conderton, Ashton-under-Hill and Elmley Castle. The villages are scattered with a lovely mixture of Cotswold stone and black-and-white timbered buildings with many fine inns and peaceful churchyards. Various footpaths lead up to the summit from Elmley and Kemerton. Superb views from this isolated limestone hill at 961 ft. This walk features a fairly lengthy ascent through fields and pretty woodland to the top of Bredon Hill. But the climb is rewarded with superb views of the Welsh and Malvern Hills, the River Severn and Avon, and the Cotswolds. Listen for the singing of the Skylark. The walk is best undertaken on a clear day to benefit from the views.

A shorter pushchair walk is possible through Overbury Park, up to the Plateau of the hill (park in Overbury village). This is not a circular walk but the outward journey does provide different views to the homeward one.

Distance
Overbury walk: 3.25 miles/5.2km, Elmley Castle walk: 5.5 miles/8.8km.

Minimum Time
Elmley Castle walk: 3.5 hours.

Grade/Level of Difficulty
Easy/Moderate

Terrain/Paths
Grass, woodland, tracks, roads.

Landscape
Fields and woodland

Dogs
To be kept under control at all times. Beware livestock.

Public Toilets
None

Parking (P)
Outside Elmley Castle church

Recommended Start/Finish
Elmley Castle

Location
Elmley Castle/Bredon Hill is located north of Tewksbury and can be accessed via the A46, A44 and B4080.

Features of Interest...

Banbury Stone. Associated with legends, witchcraft and superstitions.

Bredon Hill & surrounding villages. Immortalised by John Moore's Brensham Trilogy and by Houseman's poem 'See the Coloured Counties and Hear the Larks so High'. The hill and villages are detached from the Cotswold range but share the characteristics of the Cotswolds and Middle England; stone and half-timbered buildings. These villages are well kept and proud of their churchyards, country pubs and tended cottage gardens.

Bredon Hill Fort. Iron Age fort with two ramparts. Scene of great battle at the time of Christ, possibly against the Belgic invaders. The hacked remains of 50 men were found near the entrance. Superb views over to Wales, Vale of Evesham, the rivers Severn and Avon, and to the Cotswolds.

Conderton Pottery, The Old Forge. Distinctive salt-glaze stoneware pots by specialist country potter, Toff Milway. Open M-Sa 9-5. 01386 725387.
www.toffmilway.co.uk

Elmley Castle. Village named after the C11 site on Castle Hill. Elmley means 'Elm tree by the field'. A pretty village green.

Elmley Castle Ruins. Castle Hill, built in late C11, and refortified in C14. Little remains today.

Overbury. One of Worcestershire's most attractive villages. A mix of Cotswold stone and half-timbered houses - Stuart and Georgian. C18 Overbury Court.

Parson's Folly. Inside fort, short tower, late C18.

St Mary's Church, Elmley. Saxon and mix of the C12, C13 and C14. C17 monument of Savage Family inside. Superb sundial.

Overbury Park

Where to Eat & Drink...

The Star Inn, Ashton-under-Hill. Perfect rest stop for walkers. Children and dogs welcome. Large garden. Delicious home-cooked food to eat in or takeaway. 01386 881325
www.thestar-ashtonunderhill.co.uk

Yew Tree Inn, Conderton. One of the most popular local pubs around Bredon Hill. Conveniently situated for pre- or post-walk drinks. Basic pub grub. 01386 725364

Where to Eat & Drink just off the map...

The Anchor Inn & Restaurant, Eckington. Traditional and continental cuisine. B&B. 01386 750356
www.anchoreckington.co.uk

The Bell, Church Street, Eckington. Traditional country pub located in a rural village setting. Four ensuite bedrooms for B&B with separate access. 01386 750033
www.thebelleckington.com

Where to Stay just off the map...

Harrowfields, Cotheridge Lane, Eckington. This picturesque black-and-white timbered country cottage nestles peacefully in the Cotswold landscape. Fine attention to detail and guests' needs. 01386 751053
www.harrowfields.co.uk

Lampitt House, Lampitt Lane, Bredons Norton. Comfortable family house set in peaceful surroundings. Ensuite rooms, large private garden. 01684 772295
www.lampitthouse.co.uk

Lower End House, Manor Road, Eckington. Believed to be one of the oldest houses in Worcestershire. A period house full of character that has been renovated with emphasis on quality and style. Perfectly located for walking on the nearby Bredon or Malvern Hills. 01386 751600
www.eckingtonmanor.co.uk

Meadows Home Farm, Bredons Norton. Family run working farm in a quiet setting. One ensuite double bedroom and one ensuite room with a double and a single bed. Garden and patio area, TV lounge, ample parking. 01684 772322 www.meadowshomefarm.co.uk

Cattle below Castle Hill

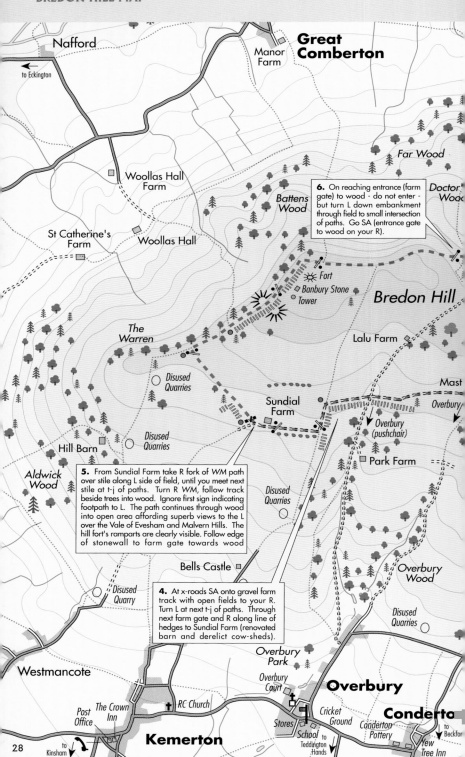

Nafford

Great Comberton

Manor Farm

← to Eckington

Woollas Hall Farm

Far Wood

Battens Wood

Doctor Wood

St Catherine's Farm

Woollas Hall

6. On reaching entrance (farm gate) to wood - do not enter - but turn L down embankment through field to small intersection of paths. Go SA (entrance gate to wood on your R).

☀ Fort
⊙ Banbury Stone
Tower

Bredon Hill

The Warren

Lalu Farm

Mast

Disused Quarries

Overbury

Sundial Farm

Overbury (pushchair)

Disused Quarries

Hill Barn

Park Farm

Aldwick Wood

5. From Sundial Farm take R fork of *WM* path over stile along L side of field, until you meet next stile at t-j of paths. Turn R *WM*, follow track beside trees into wood. Ignore first sign indicating footpath to L. The path continues through wood into open area affording superb views to the L over the Vale of Evesham and Malvern Hills. The hill fort's ramparts are clearly visible. Follow edge of stonewall to farm gate towards wood

Disused Quarries

Bells Castle ▢

4. At x-roads SA onto gravel farm track with open fields to your R. Turn L at next t-j of paths. Through next farm gate and R along line of hedges to Sundial Farm (renovated barn and derelict cow-sheds).

Overbury Wood

Disused Quarries

Westmancote

Overbury Park

Overbury Court

Overbury

Conderto

Post Office

The Crown Inn

† RC Church

Stores

School to Teddington Hands

Cricket Ground

Conderton Pottery

to Beckfor

Kemerton

to Kinsham ↻

Yew Tree Inn

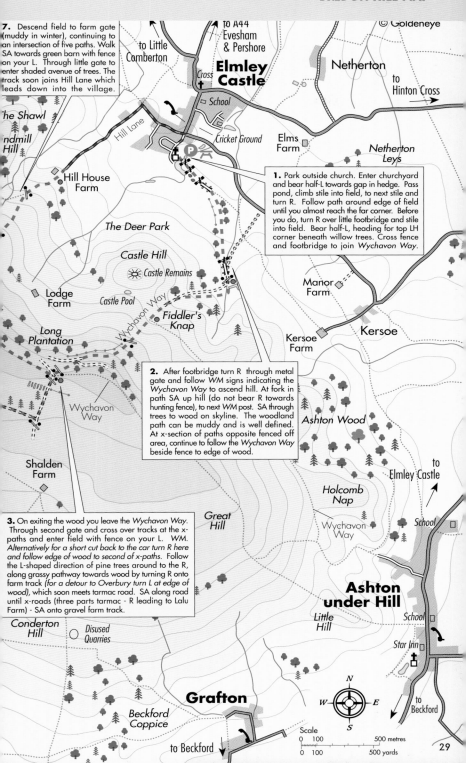

© Goldeneye

7. Descend field to farm gate (muddy in winter), continuing to an intersection of five paths. Walk SA towards green barn with fence on your L. Through little gate to enter shaded avenue of trees. The track soon joins Hill Lane which leads down into the village.

to Little Comberton

to A44 Evesham & Pershore

Elmley Castle

Netherton

to Hinton Cross

Cross

School

The Shawl

ndmill Hill

Hill Lane

Cricket Ground

Elms Farm

Netherton Leys

Hill House Farm

The Deer Park

1. Park outside church. Enter churchyard and bear half-L towards gap in hedge. Pass pond, climb stile into field, to next stile and turn R. Follow path around edge of field until you almost reach the far corner. Before you do, turn R over little footbridge and stile into field. Bear half-L, heading for top LH corner beneath willow trees. Cross fence and footbridge to join *Wychavon Way*.

Castle Hill

☀ Castle Remains

Manor Farm

Lodge Farm

Castle Pool

Wychavon Way

Fiddler's Knap

Kersoe Farm

Kersoe

Long Plantation

2. After footbridge turn R through metal gate and follow *WM* signs indicating the *Wychavon Way* to ascend hill. At fork in path SA up hill (do not bear R towards hunting fence), to next *WM* post. SA through trees to wood on skyline. The woodland path can be muddy and is well defined. At x-section of paths opposite fenced off area, continue to follow the *Wychavon Way* beside fence to edge of wood.

Wychavon Way

Ashton Wood

Shalden Farm

Holcomb Nap

to Elmley Castle

Wychavon Way

School

Great Hill

3. On exiting the wood you leave the *Wychavon Way*. Through second gate and cross over tracks at the x-paths and enter field with fence on your L. *WM*. *Alternatively for a short cut back to the car turn R here and follow edge of wood to second of x-paths.* Follow the L-shaped direction of pine trees around to the R, along grassy pathway towards wood by turning R onto farm track *(for a detour to Overbury turn L at edge of wood)*, which soon meets tarmac road. SA along road until x-roads (three parts tarmac - R leading to Lalu Farm) - SA onto gravel farm track.

Ashton under Hill

School

Conderton Hill

Disused Quarries

Little Hill

Star Inn

to Beckford

Grafton

Beckford Coppice

N
W   E
S

to Beckford

Scale
0   100   500 metres
0   100   500 yards

29

St Peter's Church Tower

It is worth a wander around the historic village of Winchcombe before the climb up Salters Hill. At first this is a fairly energetic ascent, thereafter the route is comparatively easy. The views north towards the Vale of Evesham are a delight. And as you cross the Salt Way and bear down on Parks Farm the views towards Cleeve Common and left up the valley are magnificent. Return to Winchcombe through the parkland of Sudeley Castle.

Distance
10 miles/16km

Minimum Time
4 hours

Grade/Level of Difficulty
Moderate

Terrain/Paths
Stone paths, farm tracks, grass.

Landscape
Patchwork of arable fields, sheep pastures, rolling hills, woodland.

Dogs
Quite a lot of farm tracks through sheep pastures. Keep under control at all times.

Public Toilets
Winchcombe High Street

Parking
Gloucester Street opposite Church, or in Long Stay beside County Library.

Recommended Start/Finish
Winchcombe High Street

Location
Midway between Cheltenham and Broadway on the B4632.

Link to other walks in this Guide
Cleeve Hill Walk via The Cotswold Way.

Features of Interest...

Folk & Police Museum, Town Hall. History of the town, police and weapons. TIC. Open East/Apr-Oct M-Sa 10-1, 2-4.30. 01242 609151

Salt Way. This prehistoric track runs east of Winchcombe from Hailes, south towards Hawling along Sudeley Hill. It was used in medieval times to carry salt from Droitwich and coastal salt towns, salt being the essential meat preservative.

St Peter's Church. One of the great 'Wool' churches. It is of a C15 Perpendicular design but is strangely plain, yet dignified. Not as elaborate as some of the other 'Wool' churches. For example, it has no chancel arch. The gargoyles are the one notable feature, and a circumnavigation of the exterior is advised. The weathercock is the county's finest.

Sudeley Castle. A Tudor house and the original home of the Seymour family. Katherine Parr, widow of Henry VIII, lived here and lies buried in the chapel. There is a fine collection of needlework, furniture and tapestries plus paintings by Van Dyck, Rubens and Turner. All surrounded by award-winning gardens and open parkland. The Castle is open daily mid-Mar to 1 Nov 10.30-5. 01242 602308
www.sudeleycastle.co.uk

Winchcombe. This small Cotswold town lies cradled in the Isbourne Valley. It was an ancient Saxon burh (small holding) and famous medieval centre visited from far and wide for the market, horse fair and monastery which was destroyed in the C16. You can still walk the narrow streets beside the C16 and C18 cottages, but do look up and admire the many fine gables above the shop fronts. There's a local saying: Were you born in Winchcombe? This is directed at those of us who leave doors open as it can be a wee bit drafty..

Where to Eat, Drink & Stay...

5 North Street. Set in a low-beamed, quaint C17 building, this is a small and well-run restaurant which provides a relaxed and friendly atmosphere and has gained a healthy respect from fellow restaurateurs in the Cotswolds. 01242 604566

Juri's, High Street. A beautiful Grade II listed building with vine-covered conservatory and garden provides a peaceful setting and the award-winning chef offers an excellent selection of goodies for afternoon tea. Closed M-W (except BHs). 01242 602469
www.juris-tearoom.co.uk

The Lion Inn, 33 North Street. Quite recently renovated, the Lion retains many original features; stone walls, open fires....coupled with real ales, comfy chairs, and if you desire, bedrooms with all the mod cons. A fine hostelry, that won't disappoint you. 01242 603300
www.lionwinchcombe.co.uk

North Farmcote. A working family farm producing sheep and cereals situated high on the Cotswold escarpment. Built around 1840 as a dower house for Lord Sudeley's mother, the house is surrounded by a large garden where guests can have afternoon tea. Visit their specialist herb garden (open May to Oct). 01242 602304
www.northfarmcote.co.uk

Sudeley Hill Farm. Comfortable C15 listed farmhouse with panoramic views over a working sheep and arable farm of 800 acres. Three en-suite bedrooms. 01242 602344

Wesley House, High Street. Deserved reputation for excellent food. Locals travel miles to this gastronomic oasis, and no wonder. Now, with a chic, new wine bar for the local lovelies. Five bedrooms. 01242 602366
www.wesleyhouse.co.uk

White Hart, High Street. Variously viewed as a pub or a hotel, the White Hart offers quality in both departments. This C16 inn has eight en-suite bedrooms and a bar, restaurant and wine shop. 01242 602359
www.whitehartwinchcombe.co.uk

Deadmanbury Gate

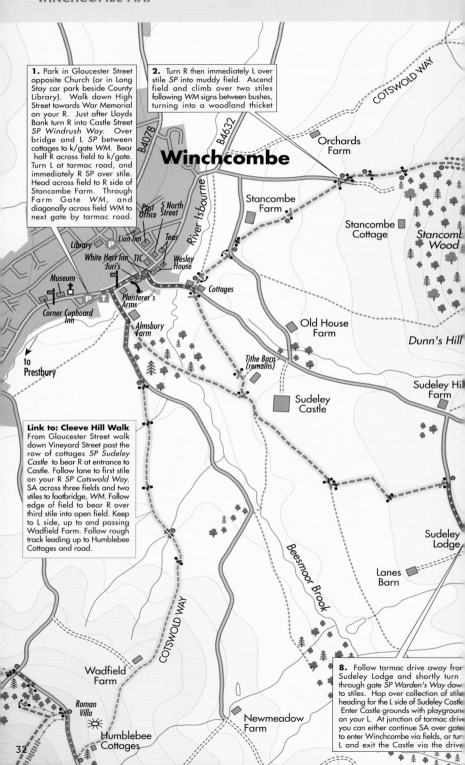

1. Park in Gloucester Street opposite Church (or in Long Stay car park beside County Library). Walk down High Street towards War Memorial on your R. Just after Lloyds Bank turn R into Castle Street *SP Windrush Way*. Over bridge and L *SP* between cottages to k/gate *WM*. Bear half R across field to k/gate. Turn L at tarmac road, and immediately R SP over stile. Head across field to R side of Stancombe Farm. Through Farm Gate *WM*, and diagonally across field *WM* to next gate by tarmac road.

2. Turn R then immediately L over stile *SP* into muddy field. Ascend field and climb over two stiles following *WM* signs between bushes, turning into a woodland thicket

COTSWOLD WAY

B4078

B4632

Orchards Farm

Winchcombe

River Isbourne

Stancombe Farm

Stancombe Cottage

Stancombe Wood

Post Office

5 North Street

Library

Lion Inn

Teas

White Hart Inn

TIC

Juri's

Wesley House

Museum

Plaisterer's Arms

Cottages

Old House Farm

Dunn's Hill

Corner Cupboard Inn

Almsbury Farm

Tithe Barn (remains)

Sudeley Hill Farm

to Prestbury

Sudeley Castle

Link to: Cleeve Hill Walk

From Gloucester Street walk down Vineyard Street past the row of cottages *SP Sudeley Castle* to bear R at entrance to Castle. Follow lane to first stile on your R *SP Cotswold Way*. SA across three fields and two stiles to footbridge, *WM*. Follow edge of field to bear R over third stile into open field. Keep to L side, up to and passing Wadfield Farm. Follow rough track leading up to Humblebee Cottages and road.

Sudeley Lodge

Lanes Barn

COTSWOLD WAY

Beesmoor Brook

Wadfield Farm

Roman Villa

Humblebee Cottages

Newmeadow Farm

8. Follow tarmac drive away from Sudeley Lodge and shortly turn through gate *SP Warden's Way* dow to stiles. Hop over collection of stile heading for the L side of Sudeley Castle Enter Castle grounds with playground on your L. At junction of tarmac drive you can either continue SA over gate to enter Winchcombe via fields, or tur L and exit the Castle via the drive

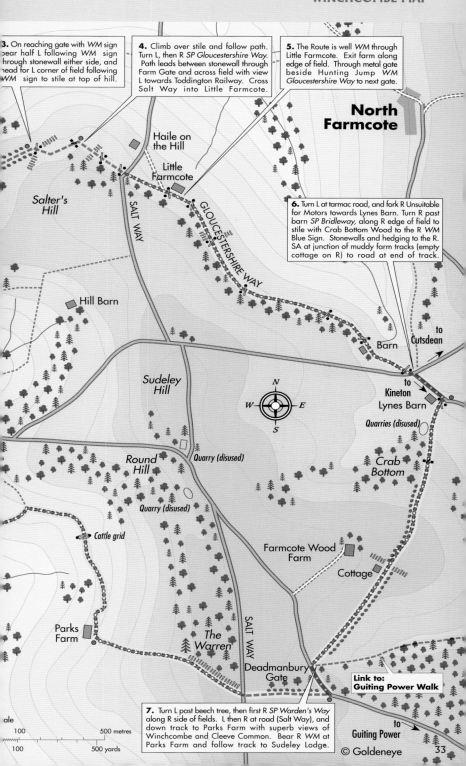

3. On reaching gate with *WM* sign bear half L following *WM* sign through stonewall either side, and head for L corner of field following *WM* sign to stile at top of hill.

4. Climb over stile and follow path. Turn L, then R *SP Gloucestershire Way*. Path leads between stonewall through Farm Gate and across field with view L towards Toddington Railway. Cross Salt Way into Little Farmcote.

5. The Route is well *WM* through Little Farmcote. Exit farm along edge of field. Through metal gate beside Hunting Jump *WM Gloucestershire Way* to next gate.

North Farmcote

Haile on the Hill

Little Farmcote

Salter's Hill

SALT WAY

GLOUCESTERSHIRE WAY

6. Turn L at tarmac road, and fork R Unsuitable for Motors towards Lynes Barn. Turn R past barn *SP Bridleway*, along R edge of field to stile with Crab Bottom Wood to the R *WM* Blue Sign. Stonewalls and hedging to the R. SA at junction of muddy farm tracks (empty cottage on R) to road at end of track.

Hill Barn

Barn

to Cutsdean

Sudeley Hill

N
W E
S

to Kineton

Lynes Barn

Quarries (disused)

Round Hill

Quarry (disused)

Crab Bottom

Quarry (disused)

Cattle grid

Farmcote Wood Farm

Cottage

Parks Farm

The Warren

SALT WAY

Deadmanbury Gate

Link to: Guiting Power Walk

to Guiting Power

7. Turn L past beech tree, then first R *SP Warden's Way* along R side of fields. L then R at road (Salt Way), and down track to Parks Farm with superb views of Winchcombe and Cleeve Common. Bear R *WM* at Parks Farm and follow track to Sudeley Lodge.

ale

100   500 metres
100   500 yards

© Goldeneye   33

Cleeve Hill

Undertake this bracing walk on a clear day and you will be richly rewarded with spectacular views of the Severn Valley, Malvern and Welsh Hills, Winchcombe and Sudeley Castle. From the Cotswolds highest viewpoint (1084ft/317metres) you cross Cleeve Common, an open space of moorland quality, along part of the Cotswold Way to a Stone Age Long Barrow, and onto a Jacobean Manor.

Distance
7 miles/11.2km. Short walk 1.5miles/2.4km.

Minimum Time
4 hours. Short walk 40 minutes.

Grade/Level of Difficulty
Easy/Moderate

Terrain/Paths
Springy turf, wide farm tracks

Landscape
Flat open moorland, undulating hills.
Sheep pastures.

Dogs
Very popular dog walking area. Dogs can run free on Cleeve Common. Otherwise keep under control.

Public Toilets
Cleeve Hill

Parking (P)
Cleeve Hill P beside toilets or by golf club.

Recommended Start/Finish
Cleeve Hill P

Location
On the B4632 between Cheltenham and Winchcombe.

Link to other walks in this Guide
Access Winchcombe walk; from Belas Knap Long Barrow to Winchcombe via Humblebee and Wadfield Farm.

Features of Interest...

Belas Knap Long Barrow. In Old English translates as 'beacon mound'. A burial chamber, 4,000 years old. Opened in 1863 to reveal 38 skeletons. In superb condition and good viewpoint. Steep footpath from road.

Cleeve Cloud. Site of Iron Age hill fort. Superb views of Severn Valley, Malvern and Welsh hills. The Ring, a site of religious/pagan rituals is just below the scarp, 100ft in diameter. Castle Rock is a popular site for the rock climbing novice.

Cleeve Common. A vast expanse of common land where you are free to roam, with dog and friends. It is more like a piece of wild moorland with its extensive horizons, and you may be forgiven for believing you are in the midst of a National Park. There are wild flowers, the Gallops (for exercising race horses) and tracks that lead off in all directions. Park in the golf course, or in the lay-byes, on the B4632.

Cleeve Hill. At 1,083 feet this is the highest point in the Cotswolds and thus a superb viewpoint across to the Malvern Hills, Welsh Mountains, and northwards across the Cotswold landscape. A popular dog walking area and, in winter snow, ideal for toboggan runs. In 1901 a tramway was built from Cheltenham to Cleeve Cloud but sadly closed in 1930.

Postlip Hall & Tithe Barn. A former Jacobean Manor House set in fifteen acres, Postlip Hall has been for the past 40 years a co-housing idyll. Eight families live in separate dwellings, working the organic kitchen garden and grounds, and pursuing their own creative pleasures, be it writing, painting, sculpting or inventing. The original tithe barn is also in continual use except when it is hired out as a venue for weddings, parties and beer festivals. www.postliphall.org.uk

Where to Eat, Drink & Sleep...

Cleeve Hill Golf Club. Public golf club perched near the top of Cleeve Hill and welcoming to non-golfers who fancy a bite to eat. Restaurant opens for lunch and dinner. 01242 672025
www.cleevehillgolfcourse.co.uk

Cleeve Hill House Hotel. Ideally situated to tackle the Cotswold Way, and or, two or three walks in this book over an energetic weekend. You will enjoy stunning views from their light and airy rooms. And, sleep the dream of rambling over hills and dales 01242 672052   www.cleevehill-hotel.co.uk

Rising Sun Hotel, Cleeve Hill. Situated close to the top of Cleeve Hill, the highest point in the Cotswolds, the views from the large beer garden are magnificent. Restaurant and bar offering seasonal menus. Children and dogs welcome. B&B. Perfect spot for a drink and sandwich on a sunny day but you may not want to start walking again! 01242 676281
www.risingsunhotel.com

View towards Queen's Wood

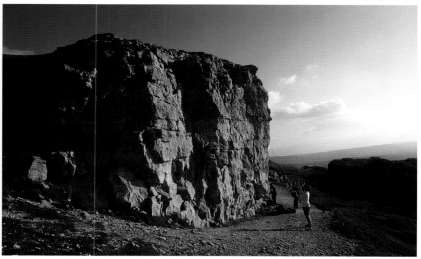

Castle Rock

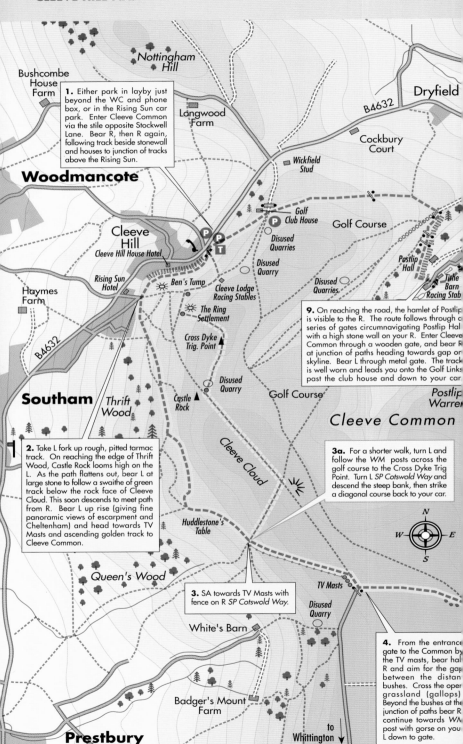

Bushcombe
House
Farm

Nottingham
Hill

Dryfield

B4632

Langwood
Farm

Cockbury
Court

Wickfield
Stud

Woodmancote

1. Either park in layby just beyond the WC and phone box, or in the Rising Sun car park. Enter Cleeve Common via the stile opposite Stockwell Lane. Bear R, then R again, following track beside stonewall and houses to junction of tracks above the Rising Sun.

Golf
Club House

Golf Course

Cleeve
Hill
Cleeve Hill House Hotel

Disused
Quarries

Rising Sun
Hotel

Ben's Tump

Disused
Quarry

Postlip
Hall

Tithe
Barn
Racing Stab

Haymes
Farm

The Ring
Settlement

Cleeve Lodge
Racing Stables

Disused
Quarries

B4632

Cross Dyke
Trig. Point

9. On reaching the road, the hamlet of Postlip is visible to the R. The route follows through a series of gates circumnavigating Postlip Hall with a high stone wall on your R. Enter Cleeve Common through a wooden gate, and bear R at junction of paths heading towards gap on skyline. Bear L through metal gate. The track is well worn and leads you onto the Golf Links past the club house and down to your car.

Southam Thrift
Wood

Castle
Rock

Disused
Quarry

Golf Course

Postlip
Warren

Cleeve Common

2. Take L fork up rough, pitted tarmac track. On reaching the edge of Thrift Wood, Castle Rock looms high on the L. As the path flattens out, bear L at large stone to follow a swaithe of green track below the rock face of Cleeve Cloud. This soon descends to meet path from R. Bear L up rise (giving fine panoramic views of escarpment and Cheltenham) and head towards TV Masts and ascending golden track to Cleeve Common.

3a. For a shorter walk, turn L and follow the WM posts across the golf course to the Cross Dyke Trig Point. Turn L SP Cotswold Way and descend the steep bank, then strike a diagonal course back to your car.

Cleeve Cloud

Huddlestone's
Table

N
W · E
S

Queen's Wood

3. SA towards TV Masts with fence on R SP Cotswold Way.

TV Masts

Disused
Quarry

4. From the entrance gate to the Common by the TV masts, bear half R and aim for the gap between the distant bushes. Cross the open grassland (gallops). Beyond the bushes at the junction of paths bear R, continue towards WM post with gorse on your L down to gate.

White's Barn

Badger's Mount
Farm

Prestbury

to
Whittington

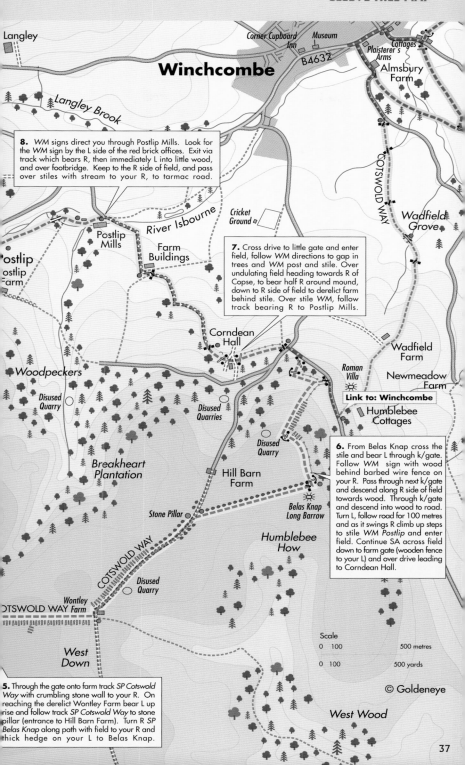

Langley

Corner Cupboard Inn   **Museum**

B4632

Plaisterer's Arms   **Cottages**

Almsbury Farm

Winchcombe

Langley Brook

COTSWOLD WAY

Wadfield Grove

8. WM signs direct you through Postlip Mills. Look for the WM sign by the L side of the red brick offices. Exit via track which bears R, then immediately L into little wood, and over footbridge. Keep to the R side of field, and pass over stiles with stream to your R, to tarmac road.

River Isbourne

Cricket Ground

Postlip Mills

Farm Buildings

ostlip
ostlip
arm

7. Cross drive to little gate and enter field, follow WM directions to gap in trees and WM post and stile. Over undulating field heading towards R of Copse, to bear half R around mound, down to R side of field to derelict farm behind stile. Over stile WM, follow track bearing R to Postlip Mills.

Corndean Hall

Wadfield Farm

Woodpeckers

Roman Villa

Newmeadow Farm

Link to: Winchcombe

Disused Quarry

Disused Quarries

Humblebee Cottages

Disused Quarry

Breakheart Plantation

Hill Barn Farm

6. From Belas Knap cross the stile and bear L through k/gate. Follow WM sign with wood behind barbed wire fence on your R. Pass through next k/gate and descend along R side of field towards wood. Through k/gate and descend into wood to road. Turn L, follow road for 100 metres and as it swings R climb up steps to stile WM Postlip and enter field. Continue SA across field down to farm gate (wooden fence to your L) and over drive leading to Corndean Hall.

Stone Pillar

Belas Knap Long Barrow

Humblebee How

COTSWOLD WAY

Disused Quarry

Wontley Farm

OTSWOLD WAY

West Down

Scale

0   100   500 metres

0   100   500 yards

5. Through the gate onto farm track SP Cotswold Way with crumbling stone wall to your R. On reaching the derelict Wontley Farm bear L up rise and follow track SP Cotswold Way to stone pillar (entrance to Hill Barn Farm). Turn R SP Belas Knap along path with field to your R and thick hedge on your L to Belas Knap.

© Goldeneye

West Wood

37

Entering Guiting Wood

A short walk from one of the Cotswolds' pretty Estate villages. Rich in wildlife, with an abundance of wild flowers and evidence of wild animals: deer, badgers, rabbits, and in summer, a profusion of butterflies. Following heavy rain the footpaths can be muddy and slippery, so wear stout footwear. These woods are managed by and belong to the Cochrane Estate, as does most of Guiting Power.

Distance
3 miles/4.8km

Minimum Time
1.5 hours

Grade/Level of Difficulty
Easy

Terrain/Paths
Farm tracks, woodland paths.

Landscape
Cultivated farmland, farm tracks, woodland.

Dogs
Keep dogs under control from parking to woods - some livestock. After that dogs run free in woodland.

Public Toilets
None

Parking (P)
Beside barn as indicated on map, or in village.

Recommended Start/Finish
From P or in village.

Location
Between Winchcombe and Stow on the Wold, west of Temple Guiting. Easiest access from Winchcombe.

Link to other walks in this Guide
Winchcombe Walk via bridle path on western edge of Guiting Wood.

Features of Interest...

Guiting Power. A hidden, somnolent estate village that surprisingly manages to support two pubs, a village shop and bakery, a nursery school and an active village hall. The blue-grey cottages belong to the Cochrane Estate (or Guiting Manor Amenity Trust) that has thankfully saved this village from greedy developers and second homeowners.

Guiting Wood.
Well tended wood full of flowers and wild animals.

St Michael's Church. Of Norman origins - both the North and South doorways are Norman. C12 chancel, C13 nave and roof. C15 Perpendicular West Tower. Severe alterations in the early C20. Interesting tombs/tablets in the churchyard. Isolated position beside ancient Anglo-Saxon settlement called Gyting Broc. Views of rolling Cotswold landscape are unforgettable.

Where to Eat & Drink...

The Farmers Arms, Winchcombe Road. Proper country pub whose exterior does not do justice to the welcome or the food served. Garden. 01451 850358

Halfway House, Kineton. C17 village pub that serves food. Small garden. B&B. 01451 850344

War Memorial, Guiting Power

The Farmer's Arms

Hollow Bottom. On the road to Winchcombe this friendly pub is popular with the racing fraternity. Traditional pub grub. 01451 850392
www.hollowbottom.com

Where to Eat & Drink just off the map...

Black Horse, Naunton. A Donnington Brewery tied house so naturally there is an excellent selection of beers on offer. A little off the beaten track so ideal for those wishing to avoid the crowds. B&B. 01451 850565

Where to Stay...

Guiting Guest House, Post Office Lane. C16 Cotswold stone former farmhouse which has been tastefully modernised. Candlelit and tasty evening meals by arrangement. Garden. Children and dogs welcome. 01451 850470 www.guitingguesthouse.com

Where to Stay just off the map...

Fox Hill, Naunton. Originally a coaching inn the Fox Hill offers annexed B&B accommodation. Children and dogs welcome. 01451 850496

St Michael's Church

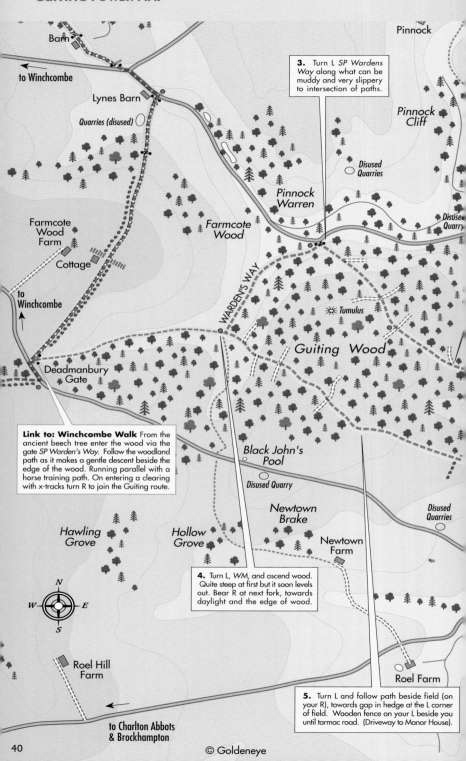

GUITING POWER MAP

Pinnock

Barn

to Winchcombe

Lynes Barn

Quarries (disused)

Pinnock
Cliff

3. Turn L *SP Wardens Way* along what can be muddy and very slippery to intersection of paths.

Disused
Quarries

Pinnock
Warren

Farmcote
Wood

Farmcote
Wood
Farm

Disuse
Quarry

Cottage

to
Winchcombe

☀ Tumulus

Guiting Wood

Deadmanbury
Gate

Link to: Winchcombe Walk From the ancient beech tree enter the wood via the gate *SP Warden's Way*. Follow the woodland path as it makes a gentle descent beside the edge of the wood. Running parallel with a horse training path. On entering a clearing with x-tracks turn R to join the Guiting route.

Black John's
Pool

Disused Quarry

Newtown
Brake

Disused
Quarries

Hawling
Grove

Hollow
Grove

Newtown
Farm

4. Turn L, *WM*, and ascend wood. Quite steep at first but it soon levels out. Bear R at next fork, towards daylight and the edge of wood.

N
W   E
S

Roel Hill
Farm

Roel Farm

5. Turn L and follow path beside field (on your R), towards gap in hedge at the L corner of field. Wooden fence on your L beside you until tarmac road. (Driveway to Manor House).

to Charlton Abbots
& Brockhampton

40

© Goldeneye

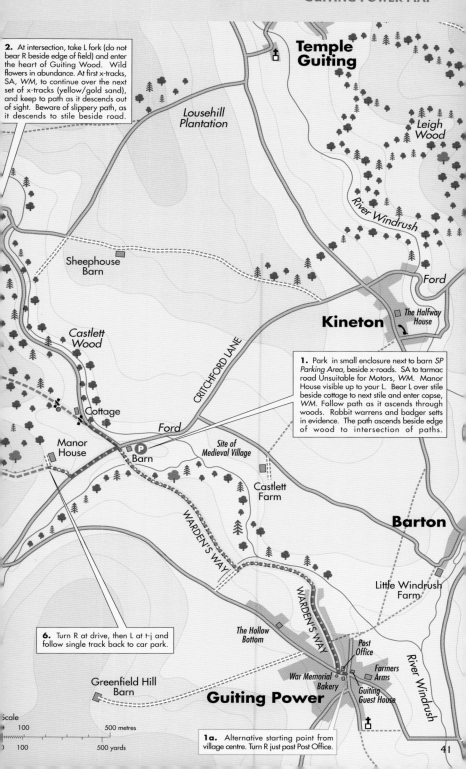

Temple Guiting

Lousehill Plantation

Leigh Wood

River Windrush

2. At intersection, take L fork (do not bear R beside edge of field) and enter the heart of Guiting Wood. Wild flowers in abundance. At first x-tracks, SA, *WM*, to continue over the next set of x-tracks (yellow/gold sand), and keep to path as it descends out of sight. Beware of slippery path, as it descends to stile beside road.

Sheephouse Barn

Ford

Kineton

The Halfway House

Castlett Wood

CRITCHFORD LANE

1. Park in small enclosure next to barn *SP Parking Area*, beside x-roads. SA to tarmac road Unsuitable for Motors, *WM*. Manor House visible up to your L. Bear L over stile beside cottage to next stile and enter copse, *WM*. Follow path as it ascends through woods. Rabbit warrens and badger setts in evidence. The path ascends beside edge of wood to intersection of paths.

Cottage

Ford

Manor House

P Barn

Site of Medieval Village

Castlett Farm

Barton

Little Windrush Farm

WARDEN'S WAY

WARDEN'S WAY

6. Turn R at drive, then L at t-j and follow single track back to car park.

The Hollow Bottom

Post Office

Farmers Arms

River Windrush

War Memorial Bakery

Guiting Guest House

Greenfield Hill Barn

Guiting Power

Scale

| 100 | 500 metres |
| 100 | 500 yards |

1a. Alternative starting point from village centre. Turn R just past Post Office.

41

Lower Slaughter

Barn below the B4068

A good half days walk that joins two of the Cotswolds most famous villages known jointly as The Slaughters. Home to Cotswold stone cottages and beautifully tended gardens and some enchanting country house hotels. The route enters, for many, unknown territory and follows the upper reaches of the Eye Stream and River Windrush. It cuts through a rich meadow of wild flowers beside the Eye Stream and crosses undulating farmland and picturesque woodland.

Distance
7.25 miles/11.6km

Minimum Time
4 hours

Grade/Level of Difficulty
Moderate

Terrain/Paths
Muddy paths, springy turf, farm track.

Landscape
River valleys, rolling farmland, woodland.

Dogs
Keep under control across farmland. Despite some sections along roadside grass verges, this walk is away from the crowds so quite good for dogs.

Public Toilets
None

Parking (P)
Beside Eye Stream, Lower Slaughter, or outside church at Upper Slaughter.

Recommended Start/Finish
Lower or Upper Slaughter P.

Location
Just off the A429 between Bourton and Stow

Link to other walks in this Guide
30 minute walk to St Lawrence's Church, Bourton on the Water.

Features of Interest...

Eyford Park. The path runs near the entrance to this C18 parkland, with early C20 house, and formal gardens. It is here that John Milton is reputed to have written his Magnum Opus, Paradise Lost. It is closed to visitors.

Lower Slaughter. Some visitors (usually Americans) to this village can't believe people actually live in these cottages – They believe it to be a film set! It is thus, one of the most popular villages in the Cotswolds, for little bridges cross the Eye Stream that runs beside the row of golden cottages. The much-painted C19 redbrick Corn Mill (see below) stands on the western edge of the village.

The Old Mill Museum, Lower Slaughter. This iconic C19 corn mill has been lovingly restored into a small museum with an Aladdin's Cave of gifts, orgasmic ice cream parlour and riverside tea room. The proprietor is a charmer, and lead singer in a Jazz band, hence the funky music. 01451 820052
www.oldmilllowerslaughter.com

Upper Slaughter. This village lies a couple of miles upstream from its neighbour. It has an impressive old Manor House visible from the road, and once lived in by the Slaughter family. Around the corner, the old Post Office with a beautiful kitchen garden. But, keep going, for along the lane past the church the road ascends to provide a splendid view of a ford and stream hidden beneath lush vegetation.

Where to Eat, Drink, Stay... And, Be Merry.

Lower Slaughter Manor. A perfectly proportioned C17 Cotswold manor endowed with a walled garden, and a unique, two-storey C15 dovecote. The hotel has spacious, comfortable rooms, furnished with antiques, and Old Masters. 01451 820456   www.lowerslaughter.co.uk

Lords of the Manor, Upper Slaughter. A luxurious, long-established Country House Hotel with C17 origins set in eight acres of parkland. Always a favourite destination for US visitors, and those seeking to celebrate a "Special Occasion". Child friendly. No dogs. The former home of the Reverend F E B Witts, Rector of this parish who wrote his famous chronicle of the C18, The Diary of a Cotswold Parson. Serves afternoon tea to non-residents. 01451 820243   www.lordsofthemanor.com

The Slaughters Country Inn, Lower Slaughter. This C17 inn has undergone many guises; Eton cramming school, country house hotel, and now a swanky inn standing in four acres of beautiful grounds alongside the River Eye. The bar is a comfy, cosy bolt-hole to rest up and sooth your aching limbs and sore shins after a slog on the hills.

Reflections, Lower Slaughter

Barn beside footpath

Upper Slaughter

River Eye, Upper Slaughter

THE SLAUGHTERS MAP

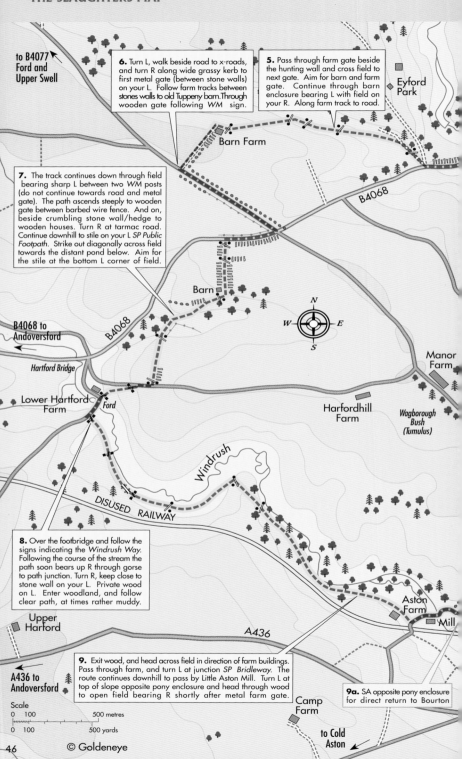

to B4077
Ford and
Upper Swell

6. Turn L, walk beside road to x-roads, and turn R along wide grassy kerb to first metal gate (between stone walls) on your L. Follow farm tracks between stones walls to old Tuppeny barn. Through wooden gate following *WM* sign.

5. Pass through farm gate beside the hunting wall and cross field to next gate. Aim for barn and farm gate. Continue through barn enclosure bearing L with field on your R. Along farm track to road.

Eyford
Park

Barn Farm

B4068

7. The track continues down through field bearing sharp L between two *WM* posts (do not continue towards road and metal gate). The path ascends steeply to wooden gate between barbed wire fence. And on, beside crumbling stone wall/hedge to wooden houses. Turn R at tarmac road. Continue downhill to stile on your L *SP Public Footpath*. Strike out diagonally across field towards the distant pond below. Aim for the stile at the bottom L corner of field.

Barn

N
W · E
S

B4068 to
Andoversford

B4068

Hartford Bridge

Manor
Farm

Lower Hartford
Farm

Ford

Harfordhill
Farm

Wagborough
Bush
(Tumulus)

Windrush

DISUSED RAILWAY

8. Over the footbridge and follow the signs indicating the *Windrush Way*. Following the course of the stream the path soon bears up R through gorse to path junction. Turn R, keep close to stone wall on your L. Private wood on L. Enter woodland, and follow clear path, at times rather muddy.

Aston
Farm

Mill

Upper
Harford

A436

A436 to
Andoversford

9. Exit wood, and head across field in direction of farm buildings. Pass through farm, and turn L at junction *SP Bridleway*. The route continues downhill to pass by Little Aston Mill. Turn L at top of slope opposite pony enclosure and head through wood to open field bearing R shortly after metal farm gate.

9a. SA opposite pony enclosure for direct return to Bourton

Camp
Farm

to Cold
Aston

Scale
0 100   500 metres
0 100   500 yards

46   © Goldeneye

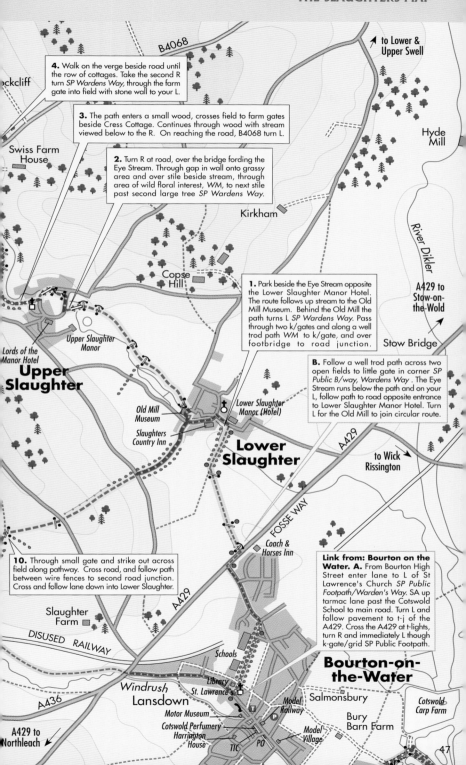

to Lower & Upper Swell

B4068

4. Walk on the verge beside road until the row of cottages. Take the second R turn *SP Wardens Way,* through the farm gate into field with stone wall to your L.

3. The path enters a small wood, crosses field to farm gates beside Cress Cottage. Continues through wood with stream viewed below to the R. On reaching the road, B4068 turn L.

2. Turn R at road, over the bridge fording the Eye Stream. Through gap in wall onto grassy area and over stile beside stream, through area of wild floral interest, *WM,* to next stile past second large tree *SP Wardens Way.*

Swiss Farm House

ckliff

Hyde Mill

Kirkham

River Dikler

Copse Hill

1. Park beside the Eye Stream opposite the Lower Slaughter Manor Hotel. The route follows up stream to the Old Mill Museum. Behind the Old Mill the path turns L *SP Wardens Way.* Pass through two k/gates and along a well trod path *WM* to k/gate, and over footbridge to road junction.

A429 to Stow-on-the-Wold

Stow Bridge

Upper Slaughter Manor

Lords of the Manor Hotel

Upper Slaughter

B. Follow a well trod path across two open fields to little gate in corner *SP Public B/way, Wardens Way* . The Eye Stream runs below the path and on your L, follow path to road opposite entrance to Lower Slaughter Manor Hotel. Turn L for the Old Mill to join circular route.

Old Mill Museum

Lower Slaughter Manor (Hotel)

Slaughters Country Inn

Lower Slaughter

A429

to Wick Rissington

FOSSE WAY

10. Through small gate and strike out across field along pathway. Cross road, and follow path between wire fences to second road junction. Cross and follow lane down into Lower Slaughter.

Coach & Horses Inn

Link from: Bourton on the Water. A. From Bourton High Street enter lane to L of St Lawrence's Church *SP Public Footpath/Warden's Way.* SA up tarmac lane past the Cotswold School to main road. Turn L and follow pavement to t-j of the A429. Cross the A429 at t-lights, turn R and immediately L though k-gate/grid *SP Public Footpath.*

Slaughter Farm

DISUSED RAILWAY

A429

Schools

Bourton-on-the-Water

A436

Windrush Lansdown

Library

St. Lawrence's

Model Railway

Salmonsbury

Cotswold Carp Farm

Motor Museum

Cotswold Perfumery Harrington House

TIC

PO

Model Village

Bury Barn Farm

A429 to Northleach

47

Bourton Lakes

First wander around Bourton and look beyond the crowds at the magnificent buildings and the graceful bridges spanning the River Windrush. And pack your binoculars as the walk passes havens of birdlife. The route climbs up to the pretty and isolated village of Little Rissington with its quaint church and golden cottages, before returning to Bourton with fine views over Bourton Vale.

Distance
3.5 miles/5.6km

Minimum Time
2.5 hours

Grade/Level of Difficulty
Easy

Terrain/Paths
Grass, farm tracks.

Landscape
Lakes and pastured farmland

Dogs
To be kept under control through farmland but generally quite good for dogs.

Public Toilets
Bourton High Street

Parking (P)
Next to Birdland, or in lay-by on Rissington Road.

Recommended Start/Finish
From lay-by on Rissington Road.

Location
On the A429 between Northleach and Stow-on-the-Wold.

Link to other walks in this Guide
30 minute walk to Lower Slaughter from St Lawrence's Church.

Features of Interest...

Bourton on the Water. One of the most popular beauty spots in the Cotswolds, but one that invites mixed opinions and is best visited out of season. It can be charming on a quiet, frostbitten morning when only the postman is out and about, but is best avoided on a busy bank holiday. You must, however, look beyond the crowds and wander the little streets for there are some beautiful houses to admire. The River Windrush flows through the many gardens, beside tree-lined lawns and is spanned by low, graceful bridges built in the mid C18. The village is built above Salmonsbury Camp, a Roman settlement. There are numerous attractions within Bourton including Birdland Park & Gardens, the Cotswold Motoring Museum and the Model Village.

The Lakes. Flooded gravel pits from the 1960s and 70s. Now utilised for a carp farm, windsurfing centre and angling lake. There is a great abundance of wildlife; plants, insects and birds.

Little Rissington. Tiny Cotswold village with C12 church that is home to a moving memorial to RAF servicemen. An RAF airbase was located nearby in World War II.

Oxfordshire Way. A long distance footpath from Bourton-on-the-Water to Henley-on-Thames, linking the Cotswolds with the Chilterns. Follows the ancient tracks of the county through meadows and woods, along quiet river valleys and over windy escarpments through many a delightful village. Way marked.

Salmonsbury Camp. The Romans' second legion of 5,000 soldiers was encamped here and built Lansdown Bridge to ford the Windrush on the Fosse Way.

Windrush Valley. A slow, trickling stream in summer, with a tendency to flood in winter. The river snakes its way through quiet golden villages to create the idyllic Cotswold scene.

Where to Eat & Drink...

The Old New Inn.
Originally a Queen Anne coaching inn, it provides traditional comfort and good homemade food. B&B. Beer garden. 01451 820467 www.theoldnewinn.co.uk

Where to Stay...

Dial House, The Chestnuts. A sumptuous and small, intimate hotel with individually designed bedrooms. Informal lunches, candlelit dinners, roaring log fires and romantic rooms are all for your pleasure, and it's nicely tucked away within a large garden. 01451 822244 www.dialhousehotel.com

Harrington House. A centre for walking holidays complete with drying room. One of the finest houses in Bourton with a Palladian faÁade with Cotswold stone roof surrounded by a domed belvedere.

Touchstone B&B, Little Rissington.
Comfy rooms in quiet village. 01451 822481

Whiteshoots Cottage, Whiteshoots Hill.
Simple accommodation with hosts that welcome both dogs and children. The house is set in three acres of garden so there is plenty of space to let children run around if the walk hasn't tired them out. 01451 822698 www.whiteshoots.co.uk

Where to Stay just off the map...

Blanche House, Turkdean. Almost 500 acres of farmland, meadows, woods and ponds surround this picturesque house. Guests are encouraged to explore on foot or horseback. Breakfast in the glass barn overlooking it all. 01451 861176 www.blanchehouse.com

Clapton Manor, Clapton-on-the-Hill.
Stunning Grade II listed Tudor house with a beautiful garden created by your host - a garden designer and historian. 01451 810202 www.claptonmanor.co.uk

Folly Farm Campsite. Set high on an exposed plateau above Bourton. Ideal for tents and the simple life. Don't expect 5 star accommodation. 01451 820285 www.cotswoldcamping.net

In addition to the above suggestions, Bourton on the Water has a wide selection of pubs and tearooms.

Bourton-on-the-Water

Little Rissington Church

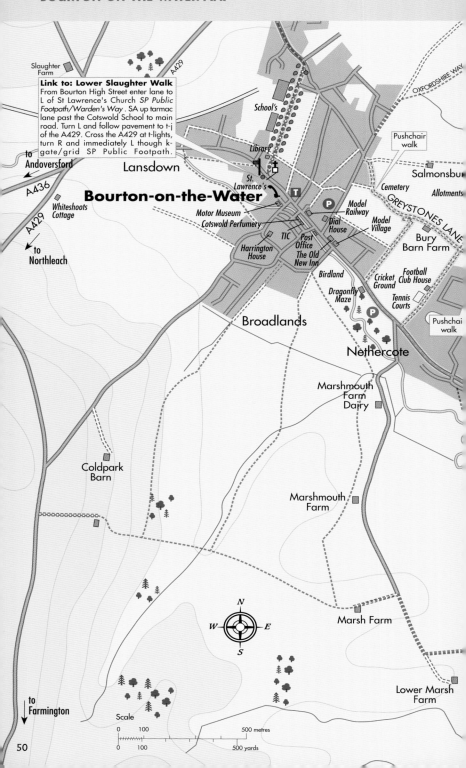

Slaughter Farm

Link to: Lower Slaughter Walk
From Bourton High Street enter lane to L of St Lawrence's Church *SP Public Footpath/Warden's Way* . SA up tarmac lane past the Cotswold School to main road. Turn L and follow pavement to t-j of the A429. Cross the A429 at t-lights, turn R and immediately L though k-gate/grid SP Public Footpath.

A429

School's

Pushchair walk

OXFORDSHIRE WAY

Library

to Andoversford

A436

Lansdown

St. Lawrence's

Salmonsbu

Cemetery

Allotments

Bourton-on-the-Water

T

GREYSTONES LANE

A429

Whiteshoots Cottage

P

Model Railway

to Northleach

Motor Museum
Cotswold Perfumery

Dial House

Model Village

Bury Barn Farm

Harrington House

TIC

Post Office
The Old New Inn

Birdland

Cricket Ground

Football Club House

Dragonfly Maze

P

Tennis Courts

Broadlands

Pushchai walk

Nethercote

Marshmouth Farm Dairy

Coldpark Barn

Marshmouth Farm

Marsh Farm

N
W   E
S

to Farmington

Lower Marsh Farm

Scale

0   100   500 metres

0   100   500 yards

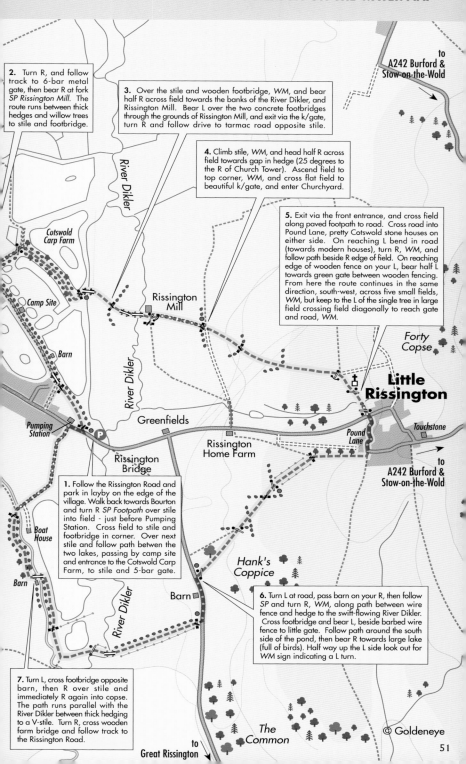

2. Turn R, and follow track to 6-bar metal gate, then bear R at fork *SP Rissington Mill*. The route runs between thick hedges and willow trees to stile and footbridge.

3. Over the stile and wooden footbridge, *WM*, and bear half R across field towards the banks of the River Dikler, and Rissington Mill. Bear L over the two concrete footbridges through the grounds of Rissington Mill, and exit via the k/gate, turn R and follow drive to tarmac road opposite stile.

4. Climb stile, *WM*, and head half R across field towards gap in hedge (25 degrees to the R of Church Tower). Ascend field to top corner, *WM*, and cross flat field to beautiful k/gate, and enter Churchyard.

5. Exit via the front entrance, and cross field along paved footpath to road. Cross road into Pound Lane, pretty Cotswold stone houses on either side. On reaching L bend in road (towards modern houses), turn R, *WM*, and follow path beside R edge of field. On reaching edge of wooden fence on your L, bear half L towards green gate between wooden fencing. From here the route continues in the same direction, south-west, across five small fields, *WM*, but keep to the L of the single tree in large field crossing field diagonally to reach gate and road, *WM*.

1. Follow the Rissington Road and park in layby on the edge of the village. Walk back towards Bourton and turn R *SP Footpath* over stile into field - just before Pumping Station. Cross field to stile and footbridge in corner. Over next stile and follow path between the two lakes, passing by camp site and entrance to the Cotswold Carp Farm, to stile and 5-bar gate.

6. Turn L at road, pass barn on your R, then follow *SP* and turn R, *WM*, along path between wire fence and hedge to the swift-flowing River Dikler. Cross footbridge and bear L, beside barbed wire fence to little gate. Follow path around the south side of the pond, then bear R towards large lake (full of birds). Half way up the L side look out for *WM* sign indicating a L turn.

7. Turn L, cross footbridge opposite barn, then R over stile and immediately R again into copse. The path runs parallel with the River Dikler between thick hedging to a V-stile. Turn R, cross wooden farm bridge and follow track to the Rissington Road.

to
A242 Burford &
Stow-on-the-Wold

River Dikler

Cotswold
Carp Farm

Camp Site

Barn

Rissington
Mill

River Dikler

Forty
Copse

**Little
Rissington**

Touchstone

Pumping
Station

Greenfields

Pound
Lane

to
A242 Burford &
Stow-on-the-Wold

Rissington
Bridge

Rissington
Home Farm

Boat
House

Barn

Barn

Hank's
Coppice

*The
Common*

to
Great Rissington

© Goldeneye

51

River Windrush, Bourton-On-The-Water

River Windrush, Burford

This is an easy, relaxing stroll away from the hustle and bustle of Burford. First, there is a slight ascent across open fields providing fine views of the surrounding countryside. Then, the route goes past conserved woodland to meander amidst lush green meadows beside the crystal clear waters of the River Windrush.

Distance
5.5 miles/8.8km

Minimum Time
2.5 hours

Grade/Level of Difficulty
Easy

Terrain/Paths
Grass, meadowland, farm tracks.

Landscape
Rolling pastureland, meadows in river valley.

Dogs
Popular dog walking spot along the river. Some livestock, however, mostly arable pastures. Dogs to be kept under control around livestock.

Public Toilets
Burford High Street

Parking (P)
Behind church, across bridge.

Recommended Start/Finish
Burford High Street

Location
On the A40 midway between Oxford and Cheltenham, or on the A361 eleven miles north of Lechlade.

Features of Interest...

Burford. The first major Cotswold town you come to, if travelling from the east, and what an introduction. The wide High Street, with its classical gables atop some gracious houses, slopes down to the dreamy, River Windrush. Once an important coach and wool centre bursting with activity. A history of civil rights and religious tolerance prevailed here with the Burford Levellers. On 17 May 1649, three soldiers were executed in Burford Churchyard on the orders of Oliver Cromwell. These three had sought to undermine the authority of Cromwell whom they considered to be a dictator rather than a liberator. This event is celebrated every year with song, dance and speeches. Today, there are many splendid inns, coffee shops (too many to mention) ideal for a pre-walk breakfast; The Priory, Hacketts, and Mrs Bumble for take-away sandwiches/lunch boxes.

Fulbrook. An attractive village of Cotswold stone with a quaint church, and two inns; the Carpenters and Mason's Arms. For those with the constitution it demands you could be forgiven for thinking this walk may very well turn into a pub crawl.

River Windrush. Seen at the beginning, and end, of this walk. The river can be a slow trickling stream in summer with a tendency to flood in winter. A very 'English' ambiance pervades its banks and meadows.

St John the Baptist's Church. One of the great Cotswold churches built in the C15 with proceeds earned by the local wool merchants. Hence the term 'Wool' church. It has a spacious interior more akin to a small cathedral. The porch and spire c.1450 are outstanding, as are the sculptured table tombs in the churchyard. Inside, don't miss the intricate medieval stained glass, and the monuments (painted figures). Open daily 9-5 except during services.

Swinbrook. Former home of the Mitford Family. Beautiful church with famous Fettiplace monuments. Swan Inn is a pretty pub beside the River Windrush, and worth a detour off this walk. Turn L at Widford towards St Oswald's church (built on the site of a Roman villa) and cross fields for Swinbrook.

Tolsey Museum, High Street. Burford's social and industrial history: charters, dolls house, objects of any rural trades..

Where to Eat, Drink & Be Merry... You are spoilt for choice:-

Highway Inn, 117 High Street. A choice of nine cosy bedrooms furnished in a mix of antique and modern styles. The Highway Inn has plenty of character and prides itself on offering an informal and individual experience akin to visiting friends in the country. Simple food made using local and seasonal produce. 01993 823661 www. thehighwayhotel.co.uk

Huffkins, High Street. Established in 1890. Cream teas a speciality. Traditional craft bakery, tea rooms and coffee shop. Open M-Sa 8-6, Su 10-6. 01993 822126 www.huffkins.com

Lamb Inn, Sheep Street. Your typical olde English hostelry: flagstone floors, low ceilings, nooks and crannies galore, fine ales, luxurious bedrooms and intimate lounges. Restaurant. 01993 823155 www.cotswold-inns-hotels.co.uk/lamb

Maison Blanc, High Street. French boulangerie and pâtisserie branded by celebrity chef Raymond Blanc. Serves drinks and light lunches as well as delicious takeaway fare. Open daily 8.30am to 5.30pm. 01993 823457 www.maisonblanc.co.uk

Swan Inn, Swinbrook. Owned by the Dowager Duchess of Devonshire (the former Deborah Mitford, the last of the Mitford sisters). A beautiful pub, in a delightful location, with a good balance between traditional and modern cuisine - worth the detour. B&B. 01993 823339 www.theswanswinbrook.co.uk

The Angel, 14 Witney Street. Relaxed, stylish brasserie in C16 coaching inn with log fires provides mouth-watering fare: Mediterranean dishes and enormous breakfasts prepared for the adventurous traveller. B&B. 01993 822714 www.theangelatburford.co.uk

Where to Stay...

Number One, 1 Walnut Row, Fulbrook. A popular, luxurious B&B with king sized beds a short walk from Burford. 01993 823782   www.bedandroomburford.co.uk

Star Cottage, Meadow Lane, Fulbrook. Sally Wyatt's is a delightful B&B embracing elegance and style a short walk from Burford. Self-Catering barn. Cotswold Tours.   01993 822032 www.burfordbedandbreakfast.co.uk

River Windrush, Widford

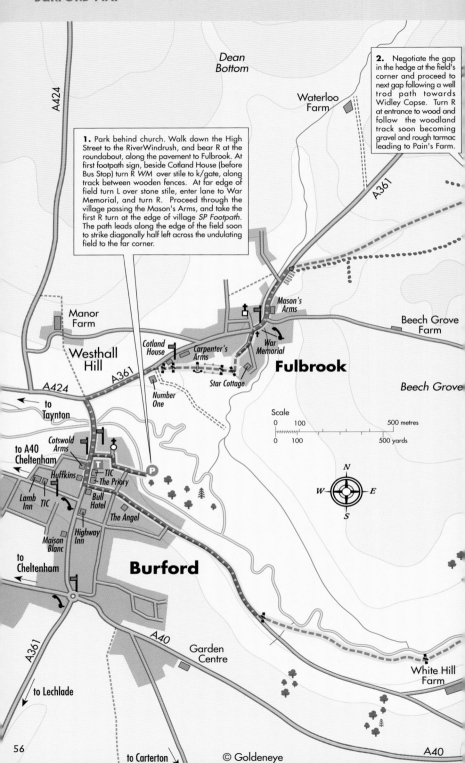

2. Negotiate the gap in the hedge at the field's corner and proceed to next gap following a well trod path towards Widley Copse. Turn R at entrance to wood and follow the woodland track soon becoming gravel and rough tarmac leading to Pain's Farm.

1. Park behind church. Walk down the High Street to the River Windrush, and bear R at the roundabout, along the pavement to Fulbrook. At first footpath sign, beside Cotland House (before Bus Stop) turn R *WM* over stile to k/gate, along track between wooden fences. At far edge of field turn L over stone stile, enter lane to War Memorial, and turn R. Proceed through the village passing the Mason's Arms, and take the first R turn at the edge of village *SP Footpath*. The path leads along the edge of the field soon to strike diagonally half left across the undulating field to the far corner.

Dean Bottom

Waterloo Farm

A424

A361

Manor Farm

Mason's Arms

Beech Grove Farm

Westhall Hill

A424

A361

Cotland House

Carpenter's Arms

War Memorial

Fulbrook

Beech Grove

Number One

Star Cottage

Scale

0   100   500 metres

0   100   500 yards

to Taynton

to A40 Cheltenham

Cotswold Arms

Huffkins

TIC
The Priory

P

N

W   E

S

Lamb Inn

TIC

Bull Hotel

The Angel

Maison Blanc

Highway Inn

to Cheltenham

Burford

Garden Centre

A40

White Hill Farm

A361

to Lechlade

56

to Carterton

© Goldeneye

A40

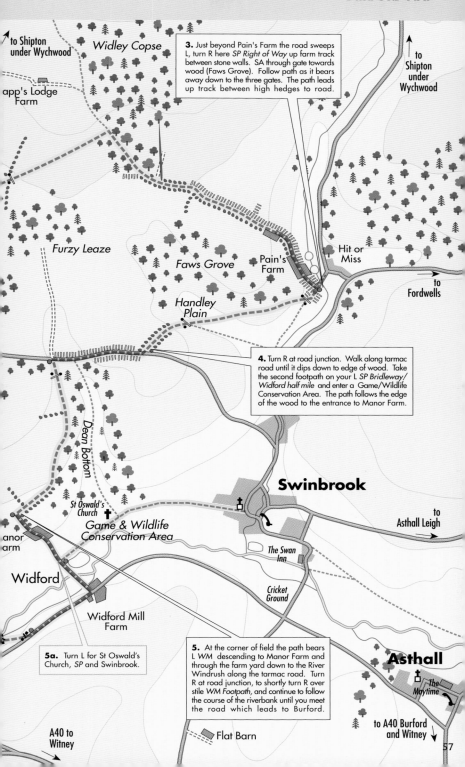

to Shipton
under Wychwood

Widley Copse

app's Lodge
Farm

to
Shipton
under
Wychwood

3. Just beyond Pain's Farm the road sweeps
L, turn R here *SP Right of Way* up farm track
between stone walls. SA through gate towards
wood (Faws Grove). Follow path as it bears
away down to the three gates. The path leads
up track between high hedges to road.

Furzy Leaze

Faws Grove

Pain's
Farm

Hit or
Miss

to
Fordwells

*Handley
Plain*

4. Turn R at road junction. Walk along tarmac
road until it dips down to edge of wood. Take
the second footpath on your L *SP Bridleway/
Widford half mile* and enter a Game/Wildlife
Conservation Area. The path follows the edge
of the wood to the entrance to Manor Farm.

Dean Bottom

Swinbrook

St Oswald's
Church

*Game & Wildlife
Conservation Area*

to
Asthall Leigh

anor
arm

The Swan
Inn

Widford

Cricket
Ground

Widford Mill
Farm

Asthall

The
Maytime

5a. Turn L for St Oswald's
Church, *SP* and Swinbrook.

5. At the corner of field the path bears
L *WM* descending to Manor Farm and
through the farm yard down to the River
Windrush along the tarmac road. Turn
R at road junction, to shortly turn R over
stile *WM Footpath*, and continue to follow
the course of the riverbank until you meet
the road which leads to Burford.

to A40 Burford
and Witney

A40 to
Witney

Flat Barn

River Windrush, Crawley Mill

The walk starts among stone cottages in the pretty village before following the river valley. At this point it can be muddy so stout footwear is recommended. After crossing the River Windrush, the path ascends through woodland. A short stretch of hedged paths and pavement leads into Crawley before returning to Minster Lovell via fields.

Distance
3.75 miles/6km

Minimum Time
1.5 hours

Grade/Level of Difficulty
Easy

Terrain/Paths
Muddy paths, grass

Landscape
River valley, woodland

Dogs
Keep under control across farmland - beware livestock. Can run free in woods.

Public Toilets
None

Parking (P)
By Churchyard, Minster Lovell.

Recommended Start/Finish
Minster Lovell.

Location
Just off the A40, between Burford and Witney.

Features of Interest...

Crawley. Tiny Oxfordshire village with Cotswold stone cottages, War Memorial and an old cloth Mill converted into separate industrial units.

Minster Lovell. Arguably the most beautiful village in the Windrush Valley. There is a fine C15 bridge leading to a street of pretty cottages and on to the C15 Church which rests beside the ancient Hall. The large open space beside the bridge is the Cricket Ground and popular picnic spot.

Minster Lovell Hall (EH). A picturesque C15 ruin beside the River Windrush. Reputed to be the haunted seat of the Lovell family who were associates of Richard III. There is evidence of medieval tracery. Associated with the rhyme 'Mistletoe Bough'. Open daily in daylight hours. www.english-heritage.org.uk

St Kenelm's Church, Minster Lovell. The church is originally Norman of cruciform design which creates a most impressive space of Renaissance proportions. Perpendicular tower. C15 stained glass. Carvings. Restored in 1870. Splendid tomb. The path into the Hall runs to the left side of the church.

Witney. This is a town of hustle and bustle with a good share of attractive limestone buildings. Note the C17 Butter Cross with gabled roof, clock turret and sundial, the Town Hall with room overhanging a piazza and across Church Green the unusually handsome spire to the Parish Church, visible from far and wide. Local history ably recorded at Cogges Manor Farm Museum.

Where to Eat & Drink...

The Lamb Inn, Crawley. Cotswold stone inn with contemporary interior and a reputation for good food. Situated opposite the War Memorial. Children welcome. Good halfway stopping point. 01993 703753 www.thelambcrawley.com

Minster Lovell Hall

Old Swan & Minster Mill, School Hill. Two buildings on the banks of the River Windrush: a C19 Mill and the C17 Old Swan Inn, with origins back to the C14 transformed into boutique-style hotels marketed towards family events and the corporate. Windrush Spa. Children and dogs welcome. 01993 774441 www.oldswanandminstermill.com

Where to Eat & Drink just off the map...

The Maytime Inn, Asthall. An authentic Cotswold building situated in a quiet country village. On a winter's day you can duck through the low door into the homely bar and imagine the pub as it was centuries ago. B&B. 01993 822068 www.themaytime.com

Where to Stay...

Hill Grove Farm, Crawley Dry Lane. 300 acre (mainly) arable working farm with cattle and free range poultry. Good farmhouse breakfast. Guests can use the garden and sunroom. B&B. Children welcome. No dogs. 01993 703120

Where to Stay just off the map...

Rectory Farm, Northmoor. Stunning C16 farmhouse situated on working farm with C18 granary building. Guest sitting/dining room. No dogs. 01865 300207 www.oxtowns.co.uk/rectoryfarm

Footpath leaving Crawley

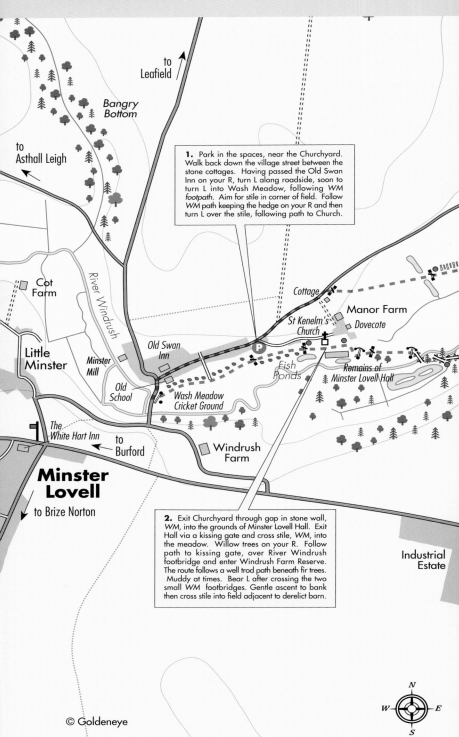

to
Leafield

Bangry
Bottom

to
Asthall Leigh

1. Park in the spaces, near the Churchyard. Walk back down the village street between the stone cottages. Having passed the Old Swan Inn on your R, turn L along roadside, soon to turn L into Wash Meadow, following *WM footpath*. Aim for stile in corner of field. Follow *WM* path keeping the hedge on your R and then turn L over the stile, following path to Church.

River Windrush

Cot
Farm

Cottage

Manor Farm

St Kenelm's
Church

Dovecote

Little
Minster

Old Swan
Inn

Minster
Mill

Fish
Ponds

Remains of
Minster Lovell Hall

Old
School

Wash Meadow
Cricket Ground

The
White Hart Inn

to Burford

Windrush
Farm

**Minster
Lovell**

to Brize Norton

2. Exit Churchyard through gap in stone wall, *WM*, into the grounds of Minster Lovell Hall. Exit Hall via a kissing gate and cross stile, *WM*, into the meadow. Willow trees on your R. Follow path to kissing gate, over River Windrush footbridge and enter Windrush Farm Reserve. The route follows a well trod path beneath fir trees. Muddy at times. Bear L after crossing the two small *WM* footbridges. Gentle ascent to bank then cross stile into field adjacent to derelict barn.

Industrial
Estate

N
W E
S

© Goldeneye

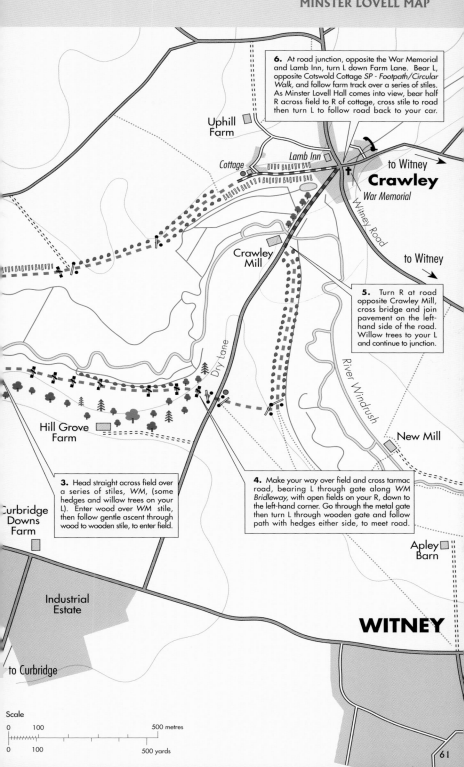

6. At road junction, opposite the War Memorial and Lamb Inn, turn L down Farm Lane. Bear L, opposite Cotswold Cottage *SP - Footpath/Circular Walk*, and follow farm track over a series of stiles. As Minster Lovell Hall comes into view, bear half R across field to R of cottage, cross stile to road then turn L to follow road back to your car.

Uphill Farm

Cottage

Lamb Inn

to Witney
Crawley
War Memorial

to Witney

Crawley Mill

5. Turn R at road opposite Crawley Mill, cross bridge and join pavement on the left-hand side of the road. Willow trees to your L and continue to junction.

Dry Lane

River Windrush

Hill Grove Farm

New Mill

3. Head straight across field over a series of stiles, *WM*, (some hedges and willow trees on your L). Enter wood over *WM* stile, then follow gentle ascent through wood to wooden stile, to enter field.

Curbridge Downs Farm

4. Make your way over field and cross tarmac road, bearing L through gate along *WM Bridleway*, with open fields on your R, down to the left-hand corner. Go through the metal gate then turn L through wooden gate and follow path with hedges either side, to meet road.

Apley Barn

Industrial Estate

WITNEY

to Curbridge

Scale

0   100   500 metres

0   100   500 yards

Group of Ironstone Cottages

The first, short walk takes you around the village past idyllic cottage gardens surmounted by thatched or roof tiles and down to an overgrown spinney. The second walk circumnavigates the Great Park, a C19 Arboretum planted by John Claudius Loudon. Bring your book on trees!

Distance
Walk 1: 1.5 miles/2.4km. Walk 2: 2.5 miles/4km

Minimum Time
Walk 1: 1 hour. Walk 2: 1.5 hours.

Grade/Level of Difficulty
Easy

Terrain/Paths
Tracks, mud, grass.

Landscape
Arable fields, woodland.

Dogs
To be kept under control at all times.

Public Toilets
None

Parking (P)
Great Tew village car park

Recommended Start/Finish
From P or in village.

Location
Situated between Banbury and Chipping Norton just off the A361 on the B4022 leading to Enstone and the A44.

Features of Interest...

Great Tew. A sensationally beautiful village lined with ironstone cottages covered in thatch and stone tiles. Many fell into disrepair but have undergone renovation. The village was designed by the Scottish architect, John Claudius Loudon. Venue for the Cornbury Music Festival In July www.cornburyfestival.com.

Great Tew Park. Planted by Loudon in the early C19. The Park has the appearance of an Arboretum.

St Michael's Church. Norman church with C13, C14 and C17 additions. Fine Tympanum and doorway. Early C14 stone monuments of a Knight and his Lady in the North aisle. Memorial to Lucius Cary (Lord Falkland). A mass of daffodils in Spring..

Cottage Garden

Where to Eat & Drink...

Falkland Arms. Named after Lord Falkland who lived here, and who died fighting for Charles I at the Battle of Newbury. A traditional pub with flagstone floors, oak beams, inglenook fireplace, mugs and bric-a-brac hanging from the ceiling, and Wadworth ales to awaken your senses. Beer Garden. B&B. No dogs or children U-16. 01608 683653 www.falklandarms.org.uk

Sweetpeas of Great Tew, 23 The Green. A florists with coffee shop serving a lazy cooked breakfast, home made cakes, hot chocs, and a pizzeria on F & Sa nights. 01608 683600   www.sweetpeasofgreattewox7.co.uk

Thatch Cottage

Where to Stay just off the map...

Swan Lodge, Enstone. C17 former inn restored and remodelled as a B&B. Ensuite rooms, guest lounge and garden. 01608 678736

White Horse Inn, Duns Tew. Beautiful C17 Inn with quality accommodation. À La Carte menu and bar snacks. 01869 340272 www.whitehorsedunstew.com

Falkland Arms

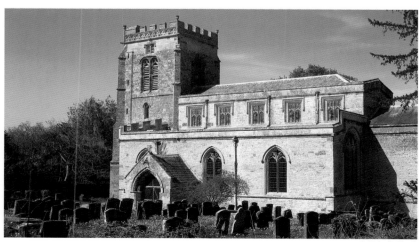

St Michael's Church

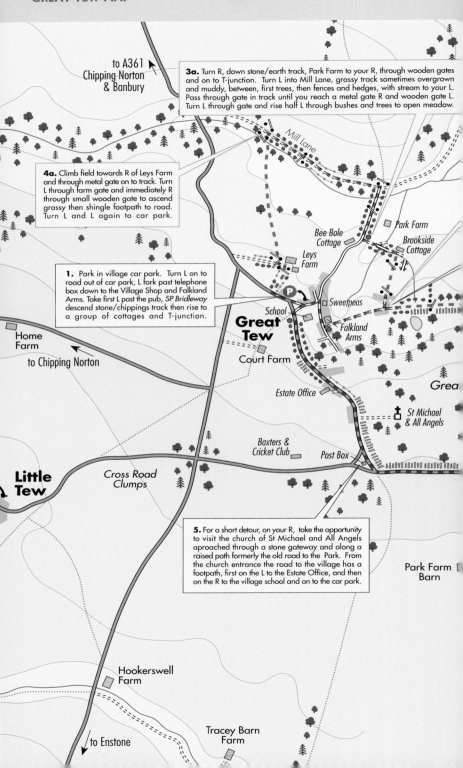

to A361
Chipping Norton
& Banbury

3a. Turn R, down stone/earth track, Park Farm to your R, through wooden gates and on to T-junction. Turn L into Mill Lane, grassy track sometimes overgrown and muddy, between, first trees, then fences and hedges, with stream to your L. Pass through gate in track until you reach a metal gate R and wooden gate L. Turn L through gate and rise half L through bushes and trees to open meadow.

Mill Lane

4a. Climb field towards R of Leys Farm and through metal gate on to track. Turn L through farm gate and immediately R through small wooden gate to ascend grassy then shingle footpath to road. Turn L and L again to car park.

Bee Bole
Cottage

Park Farm

Brookside
Cottage

Leys
Farm

1. Park in village car park. Turn L on to road out of car park, L fork past telephone box down to the Village Shop and Falkland Arms. Take first L past the pub, *SP Bridleway* descend stone/chippings track then rise to a group of cottages and T-junction.

☐ *Sweetpeas*

School

Great
Tew

Falkland
Arms

Home
Farm

to Chipping Norton

Court Farm

Grea

Estate Office

✠ St Michael
& All Angels

Little
Tew

Cross Road
Clumps

Baxters &
Cricket Club

Post Box

5. For a short detour, on your R, take the opportunity to visit the church of St Michael and All Angels aproached through a stone gateway and along a raised path formerly the old road to the Park. From the church entrance the road to the village has a footpath, first on the L to the Estate Office, and then on the R to the village school and on to the car park.

Park Farm
Barn

Hookerswell
Farm

to Enstone

Tracey Barn
Farm

© Goldeneye

1a. Turn L down stone/shingle track between cottages to wooden gate. Through gate, aim towards cottage (Brookside) at bottom of meadow. Through small metal gate and over wooden bridge, turn L along grassy footpath. Cross footbridge by wooden shed, bear L along track to T-junction opposite Bee Bole Cottage. WM. *(Turn L to return to village).*

2. Walk straight ahead, between ruined cottage and tin shed, down grassy path which becomes muddy with grotto on R. Ascend to wooden gate and into field under large trees. Open fields now on your L and stone wall to Great Tew Park on R. Pass through another wooden gate into an undulating field past a stone gateway on R, (formerly leading to an avenue of trees, now disappeared), to a metal gate. Watch out for thistles and nettles in summer in the next field, before passing a stone barn on R to metal gate.

Barn

Wooden Gateway

Hobbsshole Farm

w Park

3. Through gate, turn R on rising ground, keeping the park wall to your R and open fields to the L. Stone wall gives way to hedges and small trees in places. Pass through a gap in the hedge into the next field to a place where the stone wall zig-zags away from you. The footpath goes straight ahead with the wall 25 metres to your R but you may prefer to follow the field edge to the next gap in the hedge. The footpath again goes across the small corner of the next field before rejoining the park wall to gently rise to the road, WM.

Park Gateway

dwell Lane Spinney

Hangmans Hill

Sandford Belt

4. Turn R on to tarmac road. Park wall on your R is in better repair here and large trees overhang the road. Pass stone gateway on your R and shortly after tarmac road to L, straight on to *SP* to Great Tew. Turn R by post box and descend towards the village.

to Ledwell

N
W E
S

to Sandford St Martin

cale

100

500 metres

100

500 yards

Conygree Wood

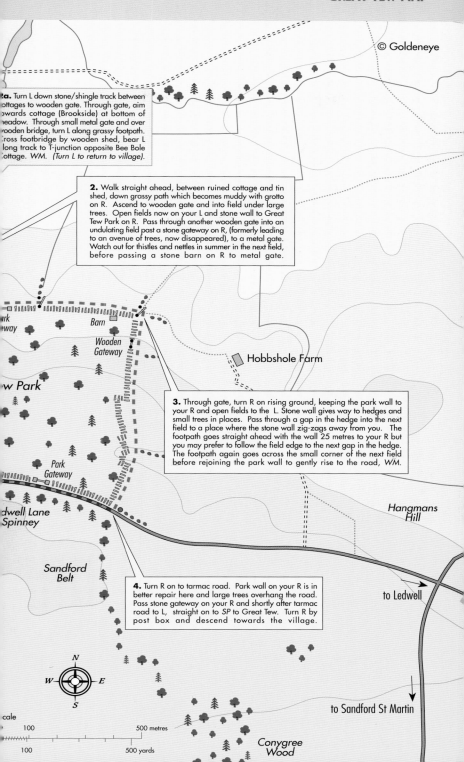

Hatherop Estate in Winter

This walk starts from a fine inn noted for its real ales and set in one of a pair of exquisite Cotswold villages situated on opposing banks of the River Leach. The route enters the Hatherop Estate and heads towards the upper reaches of the River Leach which in summer disappears underground, and crosses rolling sheep pastures beside stone walls - the quintessential Cotswold landscape.

Distance
4.5 miles/7.2km.

Minimum Time
2.5 hours

Grade/Level of Difficulty
Easy

Terrain/Paths
Tarmac, grassland, mud.

Landscape
Dry river valley, rolling sheep pastures.

Dogs
To be kept under control - beware livestock.

Public Toilets
None

Parking (P)
Opposite Victoria Inn

Recommended Start/Finish
Eastleach Turville

Location
In between Burford, Lechlade and Fairford with access via the A417, and from the A361, turning opposite Filkins.

Features of Interest...

Eastleach Turville & Eastleach Martin (Bouthrop).
Twin villages on opposite banks of the river Leach connected by the ancient clapper bridge (Keble's Bridge). The two churches were probably built by two different Lords of the Manor. In Spring, a profusion of daffodils grow along the riverbank from Keble's Bridge. Many of the cottages were built for estate workers on Sir Thomas Bazleigh's Estate, Hatherop. There is a Children's Playground if the kids still have some energy at the end of the walk.

Keble's Bridge.
Most probably built by the Keble family whose descendant, John Keble, was curate here in 1815. He founded the Oxford Movement, and is known for his volume of religious verse 'The Christian Year'.

St Andrew's Church, Eastleach Turville.
Hidden beneath the trees this tiny church has a more interesting interior than its neighbour. C14 saddleback tower of Transitional and Early English period style. Norman doorway c.1130 with carved Tympanum of Christ.

St Michael & St Martin Church, Eastleach Martin.
Founded by Richard Fitzpons, one of William the Conqueror's knights. C14 north transept. Decorated windows. Memorable exterior design and position beside the river. Closed for services in 1982.

Macaroni Downs.
Rolling sheep pastures popular as a horse racing site in the Regency period.

Where to Eat & Drink...

The Victoria Inn, Eastleach. Traditional pub grub and ale in a hostel in keeping with the beauty of its surroundings. Large beer garden suitable for muddy walkers and dogs. 01367 850277

Where to Eat & Drink just off the map...

The Swan, Southrop. This is more chic restaurant than country pub and is marketed toward the affluent London weekenders who play at country bumpkin for the weekend. Perfect if you like to spy on celebs in mufty (usually a disappointment) but you may get a crooked neck for all your troubles, and a hefty bill. 01367 850205
www.theswanatsouthrop.co.uk

The Victoria Inn

Keble's Bridge

EASTLEACH MAP

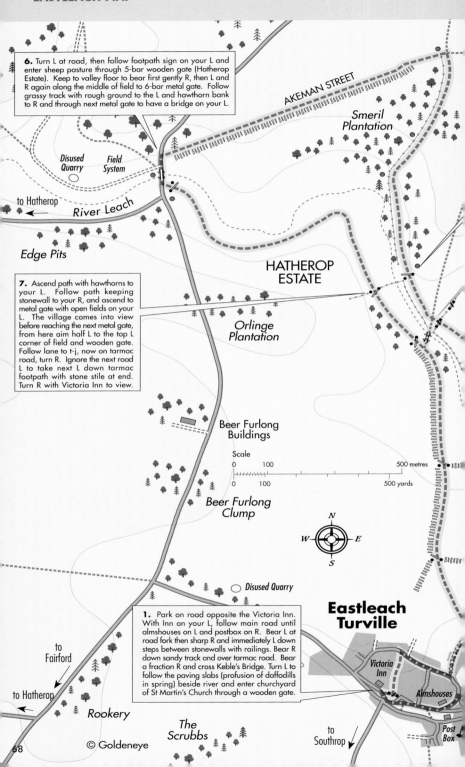

6. Turn L at road, then follow footpath sign on your L and enter sheep pasture through 5-bar wooden gate (Hatherop Estate). Keep to valley floor to bear first gently R, then L and R again along the middle of field to 6-bar metal gate. Follow grassy track with rough ground to the L and hawthorn bank to R and through next metal gate to have a bridge on your L.

AKEMAN STREET

Smeril Plantation

Disused Quarry

Field System

to Hatherop

River Leach

Edge Pits

HATHEROP ESTATE

7. Ascend path with hawthorns to your L. Follow path keeping stonewall to your R, and ascend to metal gate with open fields on your L. The village comes into view before reaching the next metal gate, from here aim half L to the top L corner of field and wooden gate. Follow lane to t-j, now on tarmac road, turn R. Ignore the next road L to take next L down tarmac footpath with stone stile at end. Turn R with Victoria Inn to view.

Orlinge Plantation

Beer Furlong Buildings

Scale

0   100   500 metres

0   100   500 yards

Beer Furlong Clump

N
W   E
S

Disused Quarry

1. Park on road opposite the Victoria Inn. With Inn on your L, follow main road until almshouses on L and postbox on R. Bear L at road fork then sharp R and immediately L down steps between stonewalls with railings. Bear R down sandy track and over tarmac road. Bear a fraction R and cross Keble's Bridge. Turn L to follow the paving slabs (profusion of daffodills in spring) beside river and enter churchyard of St Martin's Church through a wooden gate.

Eastleach Turville

to Fairford

to Hatherop

Rookery

The Scrubbs

Victoria Inn

Almshouses

to Southrop

Post Box

68   © Goldeneye

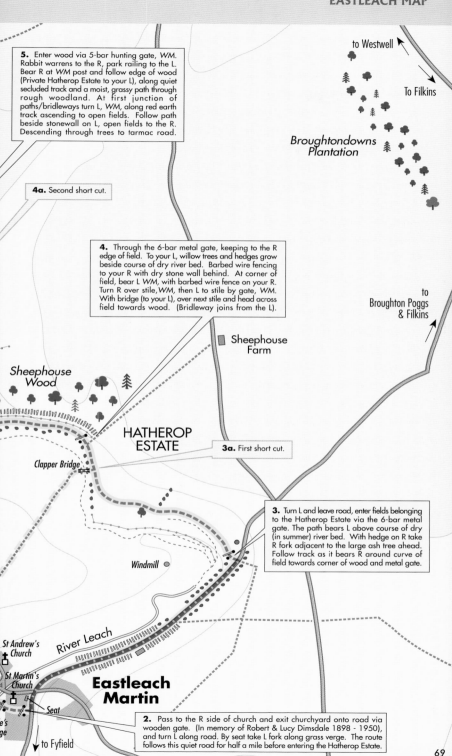

5. Enter wood via 5-bar hunting gate, *WM*. Rabbit warrens to the R, park railing to the L. Bear R at *WM* post and follow edge of wood (Private Hatherop Estate to your L), along quiet secluded track and a moist, grassy path through rough woodland. At first junction of paths/bridleways turn L, *WM*, along red earth track ascending to open fields. Follow path beside stonewall on L, open fields to the R. Descending through trees to tarmac road.

4a. Second short cut.

4. Through the 6-bar metal gate, keeping to the R edge of field. To your L, willow trees and hedges grow beside course of dry river bed. Barbed wire fencing to your R with dry stone wall behind. At corner of field, bear L *WM*, with barbed wire fence on your R. Turn R over stile, *WM*, then L to stile by gate, *WM*. With bridge (to your L), over next stile and head across field towards wood. (Bridleway joins from the L).

to Westwell

To Filkins

Broughtondowns Plantation

to Broughton Poggs & Filkins

Sheephouse Farm

Sheephouse Wood

HATHEROP ESTATE

3a. First short cut.

Clapper Bridge

3. Turn L and leave road, enter fields belonging to the Hatherop Estate via the 6-bar metal gate. The path bears L above course of dry (in summer) river bed. With hedge on R take R fork adjacent to the large ash tree ahead. Follow track as it bears R around curve of field towards corner of wood and metal gate.

Windmill

River Leach

St Andrew's Church

St Martin's Church

le's lge

Seat

Eastleach Martin

↓ to Fyfield

2. Pass to the R side of church and exit churchyard onto road via wooden gate. (In memory of Robert & Lucy Dimsdale 1898 - 1950), and turn L along road. By seat take L fork along grass verge. The route follows this quiet road for half a mile before entering the Hatherop Estate.

River Coln, Coln St Aldwyns

This is one of the most popular walks in the Cotswolds, and the reasons are obvious. It is an easy walk along a pretty river valley connecting two enchanting villages. For those with tired legs or little time the map indicates a short cut. The route is undulating and provides views of rolling sheep pastures, an old Roman route (barely visible), trout streams and rich water meadows. The views down onto the village of Coln St Aldwyns are delightful.

Distance
5.75 miles/9.2km

Minimum Time
3 hours

Level of Difficulty
Easy

Terrain/Paths
Farm tracks, woodland, grass.

Landscape
Rolling farmland, sheep pastures, river valley.

Dogs
To be kept under control at all times. Sheep pastures along riverside.

Public Toilets
Bibury, opposite river.

Parking (P)
Bibury

Recommended Start/Finish
Bibury or Coln St Aldwyns.

Location
Bibury is between Cirencester and Burford on the B4425.

Features of Interest...

Arlington Row (NT). These iconic cottages were originally monastic wool barns. However, in the C17 they were converted into weavers' homes. Now domestic dwellings, they overlook Rack Isle, a four-acre water meadow where cloth was once hung out to dry. Today, it's an open wetland meadow and wildfowl reserve.

Arlington Mill. A beautiful, historic C17 watermill beside the River Coln. Formerly a countryside museum, but sadly all the artefacts were sold off and it is now a domestic property, closed to the public.

Bibury. William Morris, the eminent Victorian poet, designer and artist lived nearby at Kelmscott and considered Bibury 'the most beautiful village in England', and few would argue with him. On the downside, it attracts the crowds and is a stop-off point for coach tours. On the up side, it is a honey-pot village made up of rose-covered cottages set behind idyllic kitchen gardens, and all overlook the sleepy River Coln inhabited by swans, trout and duckling. During the C17 Bibury was notorious as a buccaneering centre for gambling and horse racing.

Bibury Trout Farm. This working trout farm lies in a beautiful setting beside the River Coln. You can feed the fish, or try your hand at fly fishing in the Beginner's Fishery. There are fresh and prepared trout on sale, as well as plants and shrubs. Gift shop. Light refreshments. Open daily. 01285 740215 www.biburytroutfarm.co.uk

Coln St Aldwyns. Designated as one of the 10 most desirable villages in England, Coln is a lovingly cared for village of Cotswold stone set amidst a lush river valley. It is a place full of rustic charm, and featuring many of the most picturesque properties in the Cotswolds ranging from thatched Tudor cottages to Virginia creeper clad Cotswolds stone houses.

St Mary's Church, Bibury. If you seek a refuge from the hurly burly of Bibury's tourists then walk along the banks of the River Coln and you'll soon find the entrance to this pretty church. With evidence of Saxon remains, Norman font and superb sculptured table tombs.

Where to Eat & Drink...

The Catherine Wheel, Arlington. A beautiful C15 Inn with four en-suite bedrooms and pretty garden. Good food served from 12noon to 9pm. Sunday roasts. 01285 740250 www.catherinewheel-bibury.co.uk

New Inn, Coln St Aldwyns. Charming C16 ivy-clad inn delivers a combination of hotel-pub- restaurant. Efficient service, affordable cuisine and modern bedrooms. 01285 750651 www.new-inn.co.uk

Where to Stay...

Bibury Court Hotel. An impressive eighteen bedroom Jacobean mansion lying in an idyllic spot beside the River Coln. Old-style, traditional comfort at an engaging price. Open to residents and non-residents for morning coffee, lunch, afternoon tea and dinner. Dogs and children welcome. Open all year. 01285 740337 www.biburycourt.co.uk

The Swan Hotel. Few hotels have such a fabulous location as this. Overlooking the trout stream that is the River Coln. Cafè Swan (brasserie) serves light meals and afternoon tea. Fishing rights. 22 luxurious bedrooms. Dogs and children welcome. 01285 740695 www.cotswold-inns-hotels.co.uk

Cottage Garden, Bibury

Arlington Row

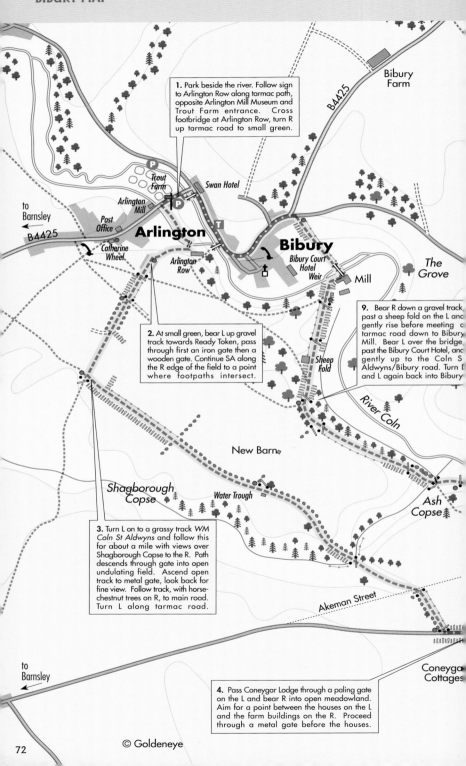

1. Park beside the river. Follow sign to Arlington Row along tarmac path, opposite Arlington Mill Museum and Trout Farm entrance. Cross footbridge at Arlington Row, turn R up tarmac road to small green.

2. At small green, bear L up gravel track towards Ready Token, pass through first an iron gate then a wooden gate. Continue SA along the R edge of the field to a point where footpaths intersect.

3. Turn L on to a grassy track *WM Coln St Aldwyns* and follow this for about a mile with views over Shagborough Copse to the R. Path descends through gate into open undulating field. Ascend open track to metal gate, look back for fine view. Follow track, with horse-chestnut trees on R, to main road. Turn L along tarmac road.

4. Pass Coneygar Lodge through a paling gate on the L and bear R into open meadowland. Aim for a point between the houses on the L and the farm buildings on the R. Proceed through a metal gate before the houses.

9. Bear R down a gravel track, past a sheep fold on the L and gently rise before meeting a tarmac road down to Bibury Mill. Bear L over the bridge, past the Bibury Court Hotel, and gently up to the Coln St Aldwyns/Bibury road. Turn L and L again back into Bibury.

Bibury Farm

B4425

The Grove

Bibury

Bibury Court Hotel

Weir

Mill

Sheep Fold

River Coln

Swan Hotel

Arlington

Trout Farm

Arlington Mill

Post Office

Catherine Wheel

Arlington Row

to Barnsley
B4425

New Barn

Shagborough Copse

Water Trough

Ash Copse

Akeman Street

to Barnsley

Coneygar Cottages

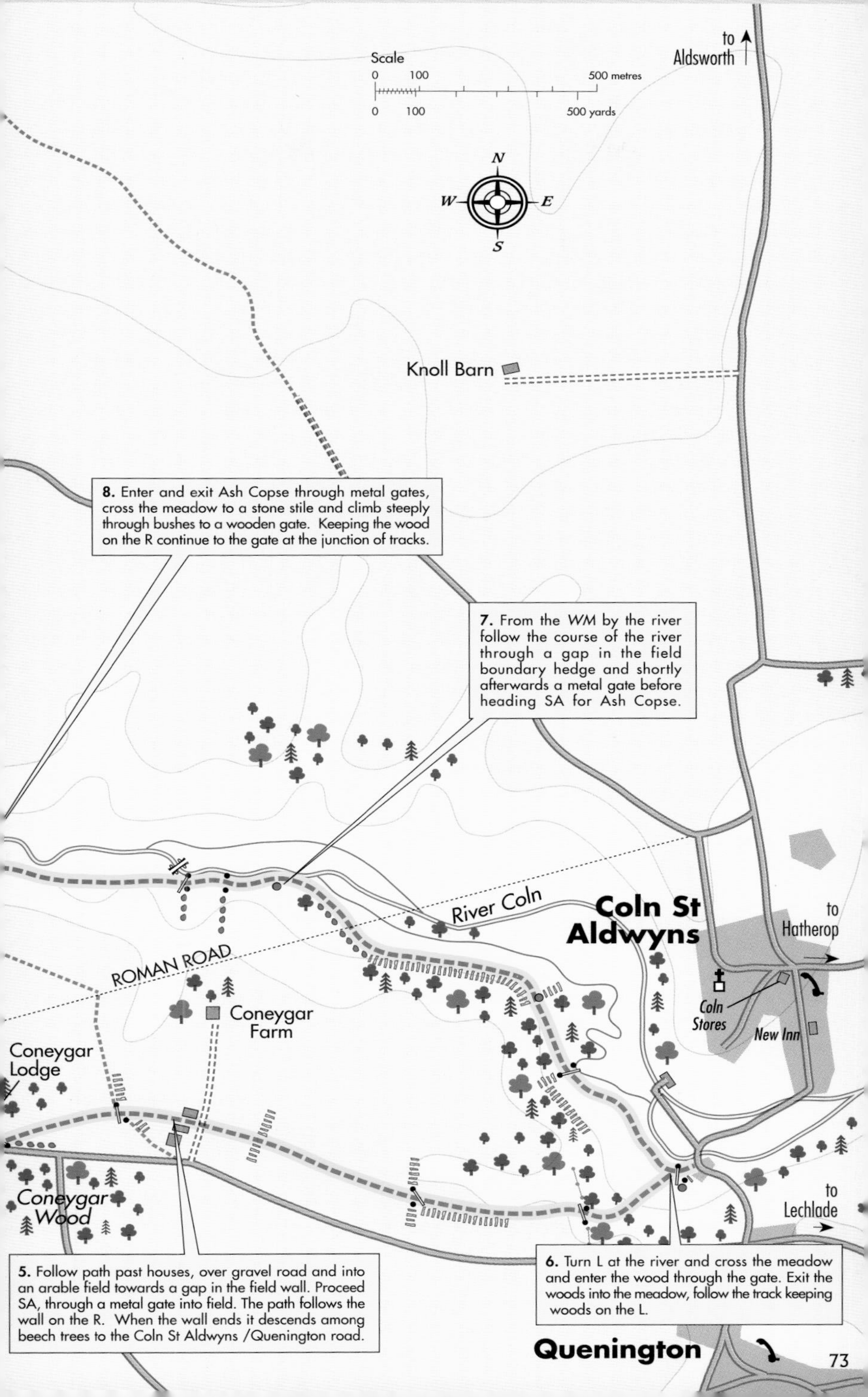
Scale
0 100 500 metres
0 100 500 yards
N
E
S
W
to Aldsworth
Knoll Barn
8. Enter and exit Ash Copse through metal gates, cross the meadow to a stone stile and climb steeply through bushes to a wooden gate. Keeping the wood on the R continue to the gate at the junction of tracks.
7. From the WM by the river follow the course of the river through a gap in the field boundary hedge and shortly afterwards a metal gate before heading SA for Ash Copse.
River Coln
ROMAN ROAD
Coln St Aldwyns
to Hatherop
Coln Stores
New Inn
Coneygar Farm
Coneygar Lodge
Coneygar Wood
to Lechlade
5. Follow path past houses, over gravel road and into an arable field towards a gap in the field wall. Proceed SA, through a metal gate into field. The path follows the wall on the R. When the wall ends it descends among beech trees to the Coln St Aldwyns /Quenington road.
6. Turn L at the river and cross the meadow and enter the wood through the gate. Exit the woods into the meadow, follow the track keeping woods on the L.
Quenington

A Misty Dawn near Yanworth Mill

This walk provides a kaleidoscope of sights, sounds and smells: Roman mosaics, the rattle of woodpeckers, woodland perfumes, cottage gardens, and rolling sheep pastures. It is mainly flat with a gradual climb to Camp Wood, then an easy descent across hunting country to Fossebridge. Finally, there is a stroll along the Chedworth valley, a short climb to the plateau overlooking the village and a descent through the wood and back to the Roman Villa.

Distance
6.25 miles/10 km

Minimum Time
3.5 hours

Grade/Level of Difficulty
Easy

Terrain/Paths
Woodland paths, farm tracks.

Landscape
Streams, woodland, farmland.

Dogs
Near Chedworth there are lots of farm fields and stiles where dogs are to be kept under control. Loop from parking through Chedworth Woods is good for dogs.

Public Toilets
None.

Parking (P)
In space 200 yards before the Roman Villa.

Recommended Start/Finish
Roman Villa.

Location
Chedworth is situated between Northleach and Cirencester, just off the A429.

Features of Interest...

Chedworth. A long, extended village in a steep-sided valley made up of five hamlets: Chedworth, Calveshill, Bleakmoor, Pancakehill and Lower Chedworth. Rich in Cotswold stone, the old cottages intermingle with modern houses. The village has a spacious ambience with fine views up and down and across the valley.

Chedworth Roman Villa (NT). Discovered in 1864 by a local gamekeeper and later excavated between 1864 and 1866 revealing remains of a Romano-British villa containing mosaics, baths and hypocausts. Family trails. Museum. Open daily except M Mar to mid-Nov, from 10am. 01242 890256 www.nationaltrust.org.uk

Chedworth Woods. A network of footpaths that criss-cross through tangled woodland close to the Roman Villa.

Coln Valley. Charming valley with the slow moving River Coln snaking its lazy way through the meadows and sheep pastures and through typically quaint Cotswold villages: Calcot, Coln Rogers, Coln St Dennis, Winson and Ablington. The Coln Valley is an example of the quintessential Cotswold river valley that meanders through green pastures, home to cattle and sheep, the moorhen and heron.

Fossebridge. Ancient coaching inn/watering hole on the Roman Fosse Way.

St Andrew's Church, Chedworth. 'Wool' church with Norman origins. C15 'wine glass' pulpit. Gargoyles.

St James the Great Church, Coln St Dennis. Picturesque. Massive Norman tower.

Stowell Park. Home of the Vestey family. Quaint Norman church with Doom painting. Gardens open under NGS scheme.

Coulsty Barn, Yanworth Mill

Where to Eat & Drink...

The Hare and Hounds. A traditional country inn with oak fireplaces. Main pub has three dining areas and a sizeable garden. B&B. 01285 720288 www.hareandhoundsinn.com

The Inn at Fossebridge. A former coaching inn conveniently positioned on the Fosseway. The Georgian hotel is set in pleasant grounds and provides comfortable rooms and fine dining as well as a lighter lunch menu in the bar. 01285 720721. www.fossebridgeinn.co.uk

Seven Tuns, Queen Street. This old pub, a favourite of the author has had a precarious existence of late. At the time of publication its future was uncertain. Let's hope it is open to assuage your thirst.

Where to Stay...

Shrove Cottage, Pancake Hill. A cosy, self-contained B&B in an ideal location for this walk, and touring the area.   Considered the perfect rural retreat. What more can you ask for? 01285 720237   www.shrovecottage.co.uk

Where to Stay just off the map...

Far Peak Camping. A simple campsite centred smack in the middle of the Cotswolds, within walking distance of Northleach. 01285 720858 www.farpeakcamping.co.uk

The Wheatsheaf, Northleach. For those with deep pockets who yearn for some luxurious bedrooms, fine dining with a twist of rollicking fun, none better than this re-invigorated old hostelry. Music Nights. Book Club. 01451 860244. www.cotswoldwheatsheaf.com

St Andrew's Church, Chedworth

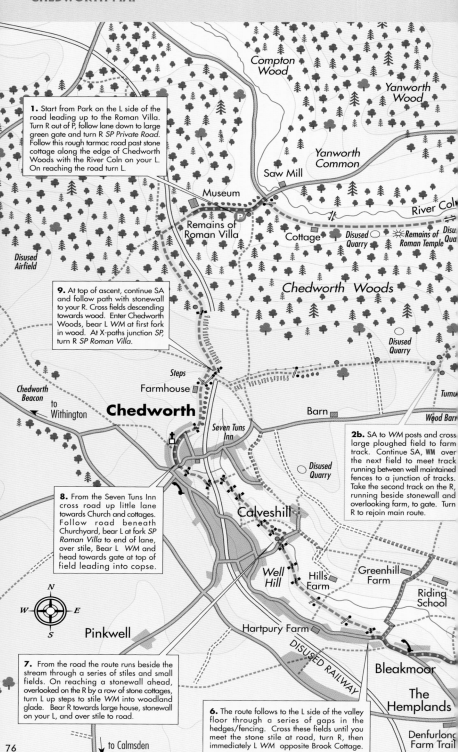

1. Start from Park on the L side of the road leading up to the Roman Villa. Turn R out of P, follow lane down to large green gate and turn R *SP Private Road*. Follow this rough tarmac road past stone cottage along the edge of Chedworth Woods with the River Coln on your L. On reaching the road turn L.

Compton Wood

Yanworth Wood

Saw Mill

Yanworth Common

Museum

Remains of Roman Villa

Cottage

Disused Quarry

Remains of Roman Temple

Disu Qua

River Col

Disused Airfield

Chedworth Woods

9. At top of ascent, continue SA and follow path with stonewall to your R. Cross fields descending towards wood. Enter Chedworth Woods, bear L *WM* at first fork in wood. At X-paths junction *SP*, turn R *SP Roman Villa*.

Disused Quarry

Steps

Farmhouse

Chedworth

Chedworth Beacon

to Withington

Barn

Wood Barn

Tumu

Seven Tuns Inn

Disused Quarry

2b. SA to *WM* posts and cross large ploughed field to farm track. Continue SA, WM over the next field to meet track running between well maintained fences to a junction of tracks. Take the second track on the R, running beside stonewall and overlooking farm, to gate. Turn R to rejoin main route.

8. From the Seven Tuns Inn cross road up little lane towards Church and cottages. Follow road beneath Churchyard, bear L at fork *SP Roman Villa* to end of lane, over stile, Bear L *WM* and head towards gate at top of field leading into copse.

Calveshill

Well Hill

Hills Farm

Greenhill Farm

Riding School

N
W — E
S

Pinkwell

Hartpury Farm

DISUSED RAILWAY

Bleakmoor

The Hemplands

7. From the road the route runs beside the stream through a series of stiles and small fields. On reaching a stonewall ahead, overlooked on the R by a row of stone cottages, turn L up steps to stile *WM* into woodland glade. Bear R towards large house, stonewall on your L, and over stile to road.

6. The route follows to the L side of the valley floor through a series of gaps in the hedges/fencing. Cross these fields until you meet the stone stile at road, turn R, then immediately L *WM* opposite Brook Cottage.

Denfurlon Farm Trail

↓ to Calmsden

76

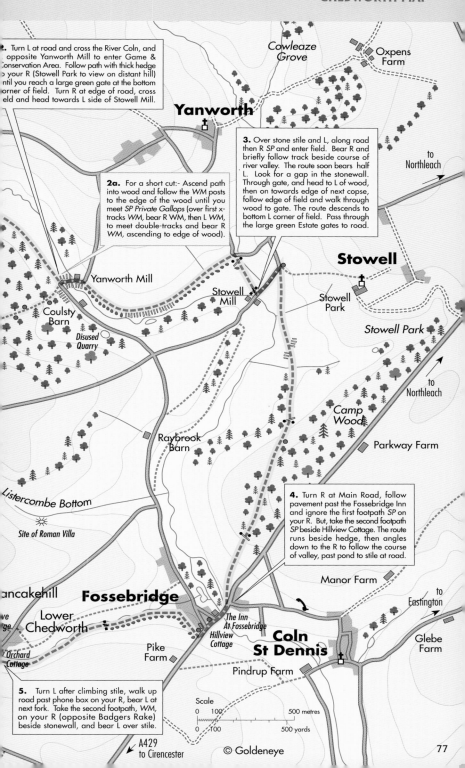

Cowleaze Grove

Oxpens Farm

2. Turn L at road and cross the River Coln, and opposite Yanworth Mill to enter Game & Conservation Area. Follow path with thick hedge to your R (Stowell Park to view on distant hill) until you reach a large green gate at the bottom corner of field. Turn R at edge of road, cross field and head towards L side of Stowell Mill.

Yanworth

to Northleach

3. Over stone stile and L, along road then R *SP* and enter field. Bear R and briefly follow track beside course of river valley. The route soon bears half L. Look for a gap in the stonewall. Through gate, and head to L of wood, then on towards edge of next copse, follow edge of field and walk through wood to gate. The route descends to bottom L corner of field. Pass through the large green Estate gates to road.

2a. For a short cut:- Ascend path into wood and follow the *WM* posts to the edge of the wood until you meet *SP Private Gallops* (over first x-tracks *WM*, bear R *WM*, then L *WM*, to meet double-tracks and bear R *WM*, ascending to edge of wood).

Stowell

Yanworth Mill

Stowell Mill

Stowell Park

Stowell Park

Coulsty Barn

Disused Quarry

to Northleach

Camp Wood

Parkway Farm

Raybrook Barn

Listercombe Bottom

Site of Roman Villa

4. Turn R at Main Road, follow pavement past the Fossebridge Inn and ignore the first footpath *SP* on your R. But, take the second footpath *SP* beside Hillview Cottage. The route runs beside hedge, then angles down to the R to follow the course of valley, past pond to stile at road.

Manor Farm

to Eastington

ancakehill

Fossebridge

Lower Chedworth

The Inn At Fossebridge

Hillview Cottage

Coln St Dennis

Glebe Farm

Orchard Cottage

Pike Farm

Pindrup Farm

5. Turn L after climbing stile, walk up road past phone box on your R, bear L at next fork. Take the second footpath, *WM*, on your R (opposite Badgers Rake) beside stonewall, and bear L over stile.

Scale
0   100   500 metres
0   100   500 yards

A429
to Cirencester

© Goldeneye

Edgeworth

The Edgeworth walk explores much of the rolling countryside of the Golden Valley, and its isolation provides solitude. The Misarden Park walk is designed for young families with pushchairs. One long descent, followed by three short climbs in rolling parkland and ancient woodland. The link between the two walks has one very steep descent in woodland and is a reminder of the wonder of Gloucestershire's trees.

Distance
Edgeworth: 2.5 miles/4km.
Misarden Park: 1.5 miles/2.4km.

Minimum Time
Edgeworth: 2.5 hours. Misarden Park: 1.5 hours.

Grade/Level of Difficulty
Both Easy

Terrain/Paths
Edgeworth: Grass, woodland track.
Misarden Park: Tarmac, grass track.

Landscape
Woodland, rolling pastureland.

Dogs
The Edgeworth walk has more woodland. Lots of sheep in Misarden Park - dogs to be kept under control.

Public Toilets
None

Parking (P)
Edgeworth: Beside Village Hall.
Misarden Park: Beside School.

Recommended Start/Finish
From Car Parks as above

Location
Edgeworth is close to Miserden, located near Birdlip, Cirencester and Stroud. The easiest access is either via the A419 from Cirencester (via Sapperton/Daneway), or from the East via the A417 through Duntisbourne Abbots.

Link between both these walks
Allow 45 minutes to join the Edgeworth section from Miserden.

Features of Interest...

Edgeworth. Situated in an isolated position overlooking the River Frome, and the upper reaches of the Stroud valleys.

Edgeworth Manor. Formerly the home of Paul Hamlyn, book publisher and philanthropist.

Misarden Park Gardens, Miserden. The home of the Wills family, of tobacco fame, has shrubs, a traditional rose garden, perennial borders, extensive yew topiary, magnolia Goulangeana and spring bulbs amidst a picturesque woodland setting. Rill and Summerhouse. The Elizabethan mansion has mullion windows and was extended by Waterhouses in the C19 and by Lutyens who added a new wing in 1920-21. The gardens are open Apr to Sept Tu, W & Th, 10-4.30. Nursery open daily except M, Apr to mid-Oct. 01285 821303 www.misardenpark.co.uk

Miserden. Estate village overlooking the Golden Valley. John Barnes built many of the estate cottages in 1920.

St Andrew's Church, Miserden. Late Saxon in origin, with a Norman font and windows. Some C16 tombs in churchyard. Sadly much was destroyed by the amateur architect, the Reverend W H Lowder, in 1886. Note the War Memorial by Lutyens and the beech and yew trees.

St Mary's Church, Edgeworth. Early Saxon with some Norman additions: nave, chancel and south door. A restored C13 porch and C14 stained glass. Look for the cross in the churchyard with medieval base and mutilated head.

Where to Eat & Drink...

Carpenter's Arms, Miserden. This old inn retains its Inglenook fireplaces and original stone floors. The village is very popular with film crews. Beer garden. Dogs welcome. 01285 821283

Where to Eat & Drink just off the map...

Bear at Bisley. Bisley's oldest pub is traditional and friendly. Bar is well stocked with a range of traditional ales. 01452 770265 www.bisleybear.co.uk

Where to Stay just off the map...

Dix's Barn, Duntisbourne Abbots. This converted barn overlooks the Area of Outstanding Natural Beauty. Fishing and riding nearby. 01285 821249

Manor Farm, Middle Duntisbourne. B&B and self-catering accommodation. 01285 658145 www.duntisbourne.com

Nation House B&B, 3 George Street, Bisley. Three cottages knocked into one makes for a splendid home and warm-hearted welcome. Family, double and single rooms available. 01452 770197

Winston Glebe B&B, Winstone. This small Georgian rectory provides traditional hospitality and English country house comforts. Dinner cooked by a former Cordon Bleu chef is a welcome option. 01285 821451 www.winstoneglebe.com

St Andrew's Churchyard, Miserden

Spring Blossom, Misarden Park

Misarden Park

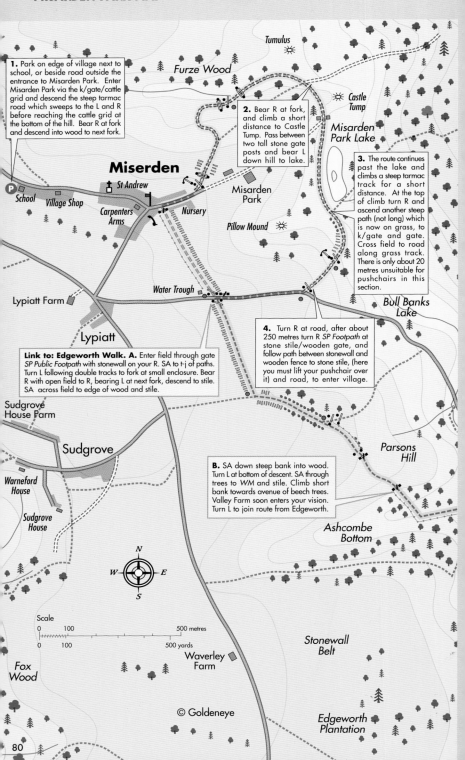

Miserden

St Andrew

School

Village Shop

Carpenters Arms

Nursery

Misarden Park

Pillow Mound

Water Trough

Lypiatt Farm

Lypiatt

Sudgrove House Farm

Sudgrove

Warneford House

Sudgrove House

Tumulus

Furze Wood

Castle Tump

Misarden Park Lake

Bull Banks Lake

Parsons Hill

Ashcombe Bottom

Stonewall Belt

Fox Wood

Waverley Farm

Edgeworth Plantation

1. Park on edge of village next to school, or beside road outside the entrance to Misarden Park. Enter Misarden Park via the k/gate/cattle grid and descend the steep tarmac road which sweeps to the L and R before reaching the cattle grid at the bottom of the hill. Bear R at fork and descend into wood to next fork.

2. Bear R at fork, and climb a short distance to Castle Tump. Pass between two tall stone gate posts and bear L down hill to lake.

3. The route continues past the lake and climbs a steep tarmac track for a short distance. At the top of climb turn R and ascend another steep path (not long) which is now on grass, to k/gate and gate. Cross field to road along grass track. There is only about 20 metres unsuitable for pushchairs in this section.

4. Turn R at road, after about 250 metres turn R *SP Footpath* at stone stile/wooden gate, and follow path between stonewall and wooden fence to stone stile, (here you must lift your pushchair over it) and road, to enter village.

Link to: Edgeworth Walk. A. Enter field through gate *SP Public Footpath* with stonewall on your R. SA to t-j of paths. Turn L following double tracks to fork at small enclosure. Bear R with open field to R, bearing L at next fork, descend to stile. SA across field to edge of wood and stile.

B. SA down steep bank into wood. Turn L at bottom of descent. SA through trees to *WM* and stile. Climb short bank towards avenue of beech trees. Valley Farm soon enters your vision. Turn L to join route from Edgeworth.

Scale

0 — 100 — 500 metres

0 — 100 — 500 yards

N / E / S / W

© Goldeneye

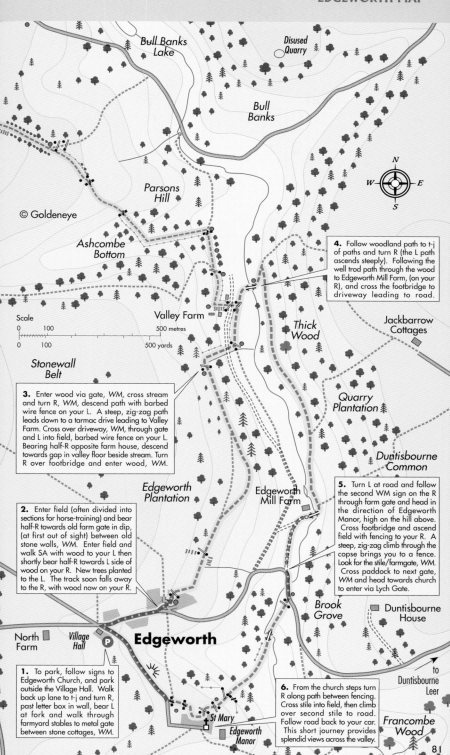

Bull Banks Lake

Disused Quarry

Bull Banks

Parsons Hill

© Goldeneye

Ashcombe Bottom

Valley Farm

N
W — E
S

4. Follow woodland path to t-j of paths and turn R (the L path ascends steeply). Following the well trod path through the wood to Edgeworth Mill Farm, (on your R), and cross the footbridge to driveway leading to road.

Thick Wood

Jackbarrow Cottages

Scale
0   100
0   100
500 metres
500 yards

Stonewall Belt

Quarry Plantation

Duntisbourne Common

3. Enter wood via gate, *WM*, cross stream and turn R, *WM*, descend path with barbed wire fence on your L. A steep, zig-zag path leads down to a tarmac drive leading to Valley Farm. Cross over driveway, *WM*, through gate and L into field, barbed wire fence on your L. Bearing half-R opposite farm house, descend towards gap in valley floor beside stream. Turn R over footbridge and enter wood, *WM*.

Edgeworth Plantation

Edgeworth Mill Farm

5. Turn L at road and follow the second WM sign on the R through farm gate and head in the direction of Edgeworth Manor, high on the hill above. Cross footbridge and ascend field with fencing to your R. A steep, zig-zag climb through the copse brings you to a fence. Look for the stile/farmgate, *WM*. Cross paddock to next gate, *WM* and head towards church to enter via Lych Gate.

2. Enter field (often divided into sections for horse-training) and bear half-R towards old farm gate in dip, (at first out of sight) between old stone walls, *WM*. Enter field and walk SA with wood to your L then shortly bear half-R towards L side of wood on your R. New trees planted to the L. The track soon falls away to the R, with wood now on your R.

Brook Grove

Duntisbourne House

North Farm

Village Hall

Edgeworth

to Duntisbourne Leer

1. To park, follow signs to Edgeworth Church, and park outside the Village Hall. Walk back up lane to t-j and turn R, past letter box in wall, bear L at fork and walk through farmyard stables to metal gate between stone cottages, *WM*.

6. From the church steps turn R along path between fencing. Cross stile into field, then climb over second stile to road. Follow road back to your car. This short journey provides splendid views across the valley.

St Mary

Edgeworth Manor

Francombe Wood

81

The Bell at Sapperton

This walk provides splendid views from Sapperton over the Golden Valley and woodlands below. Then it follows the Golden Valley beside the Thames and Severn Canal, passing by nature reserves, wild flowers, areas rich in industrial heritage and water courses set aside for freshwater habitats. There are a couple of steep climbs which will create a thirst to be slaked in one of the two fine pubs, en route.

Distance
4.25 miles/6.75km

Minimum Time
2.5 hours

Grade/Level of Difficulty
Easy/Moderate

Terrain/Paths
Mud, canal path, woodland tracks.

Landscape
Woodland, pastureland.

Dogs
Mostly woodland where dogs can run free.

Public Toilets
None

Parking (P)
Beside Sapperton church, or at the Daneway.

Recommended Start/Finish
As above

Location
Just off the A419 between Stroud and Cirencester.

Features of Interest...

Daneway Banks Nature Reserve. Regeneration of freshwater habitats. Wildflowers abound, notably the 'Lilies of the Valley'.

Daneway House. Small C14 manor. A workshop and showroom was set up here in 1902 by Ernest Gimson and the Barnsley Brothers of the "Arts & Crafts Movement" rented from the Bathurst Estate.

Daneway Portal. Entrance to the Sapperton Tunnel built in 1874-89. At the time the longest canal tunnel built for the Thames and Severn Canal which linked the Stroudwater to the Thames. The Cotswold Canal Trust are actively restoring it, and thereby creating freshwater habitats.

Golden Valley. Runs from Sapperton to Chalford; superb autumnal colours from the beech, ash and oak trees.

Pinbury Park. John Masefield, Poet Laureate lived here during World War II.

Sapperton. In a splendid position overlooking woodland and the Golden Valley. Home of the William Morris protégés, Ernest Gimson and Sydney and Ernest Barnsley of the Cotswold Arts and Crafts Movement, creators of beautiful furniture who also built their own cottages in the village. Their fame rose after completing restorative work at nearby Pinbury Park. Ernest Gimson died young at 59 and is buried in the churchyard. The area is rich in industrial heritage, woodland and circular walks. Charles I stayed at Sapperton House on 13 July, 1644.

St Kenelm's Church. Of Norman origins with elaborately carved oak panels supplied from the Manor House. Exquisite kneelers. Effigy of a C16 Knight. Monument to Sir Henry Poole, and wife.

Where to Eat & Drink...

The Bell at Sapperton. A popular dining pub with the chattering classes given to natural stonewalls, polished flagstone floors, and in winter, welcome log fires provide a comfortable ambience. Local beers. Al fresco in summer. Recipient of one of Adrian Gill's hilarious reviews in the Sunday Times. 01285 760298   www.bellsapperton.co.uk

The Daneway. Charming, traditional country pub with a reputation for giving visitors a friendly welcome. Alongside, a basic camping field in a tranquil wooded valley. Toilet and water tap at the pub. 01285 760297 www.thedaneway.com

Where to Stay just off the map...

Mayfield Park, Cirencester. Set on the north side of Cirencester this popular site welcomes tents and caravans. Open all year. 01285 831301 www.mayfieldpark.co.uk

No.12 Park Street, Cirencester. If style and gracious comfort is to your liking then this Grade II Georgian townhouse offering luxurious B&B may be just what you are looking for. 01285 640232 www.no12cirencester.co.uk

Tunnel House Inn, Coates. A rural pub with a great ambience, fine ales and yummy food has a number of small camping pitches and is located in an ideal spot beside the Thames and Severn Canal. Childrens play area. Dogs welcome. 01285 770280.   www.tunnelhouse.com

Siccaridge Wood

Wood Carving, St Kenelm's Church

SAPPERTON MAP

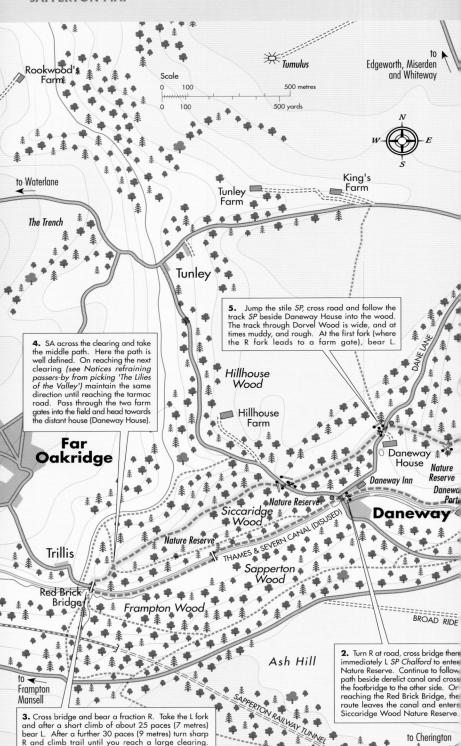

Rookwood's Farm

Tumulus

to Edgeworth, Miserden and Whiteway

Scale

0   100   500 metres

0   100   500 yards

N
W   E
S

to Waterlane

The Trench

Tunley Farm

King's Farm

Tunley

5. Jump the stile *SP*, cross road and follow the track *SP* beside Daneway House into the wood. The track through Dorvel Wood is wide, and at times muddy, and rough. At the first fork (where the R fork leads to a farm gate), bear L.

4. SA across the clearing and take the middle path. Here the path is well defined. On reaching the next clearing *(see Notices refraining passers-by from picking 'The Lilies of the Valley')* maintain the same direction until reaching the tarmac road. Pass through the two farm gates into the field and head towards the distant house (Daneway House).

Hillhouse Wood

DANE LANE

Hillhouse Farm

Far Oakridge

Daneway House

Nature Reserve

Daneway Inn

Daneway Port

Nature Reserve

Daneway

Siccaridge Wood

Nature Reserve

Trillis

THAMES & SEVERN CANAL (DISUSED)

Sapperton Wood

Red Brick Bridge

Frampton Wood

BROAD RIDE

2. Turn R at road, cross bridge then immediately L *SP Chalford* to enter Nature Reserve. Continue to follow path beside derelict canal and cross the footbridge to the other side. Or reaching the Red Brick Bridge, the route leaves the canal and enters Siccaridge Wood Nature Reserve.

Ash Hill

to Frampton Mansell

SAPPERTON RAILWAY TUNNEL

3. Cross bridge and bear a fraction R. Take the L fork and after a short climb of about 25 paces (7 metres) bear L. After a further 30 paces (9 metres) turn sharp R and climb trail until you reach a large clearing.

to Cherington

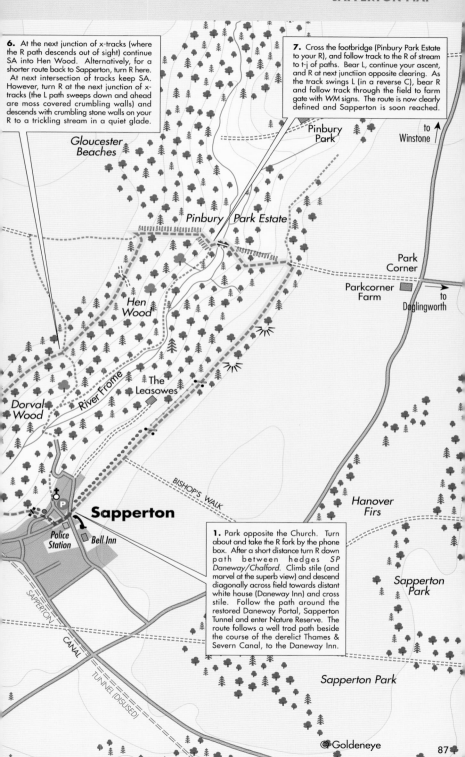

6. At the next junction of x-tracks (where the R path descends out of sight) continue SA into Hen Wood. Alternatively, for a shorter route back to Sapperton, turn R here. At next intersection of tracks keep SA. However, turn R at the next junction of x-tracks (the L path sweeps down and ahead are moss covered crumbling walls) and descends with crumbling stone walls on your R to a trickling stream in a quiet glade.

7. Cross the footbridge (Pinbury Park Estate to your R), and follow track to the R of stream to t-j of paths. Bear L, continue your ascent, and R at next junction opposite clearing. As the track swings L (in a reverse C), bear R and follow track through the field to farm gate with WM signs. The route is now clearly defined and Sapperton is soon reached.

Gloucester Beaches

Pinbury Park

to Winstone

Pinbury Park Estate

Park Corner

Parkcorner Farm

to Daglingworth

Hen Wood

Dorval Wood

River Frome

The Leasowes

BISHOP'S WALK

Hanover Firs

Sapperton

Police Station

Bell Inn

Sapperton Park

1. Park opposite the Church. Turn about and take the R fork by the phone box. After a short distance turn R down path between hedges *SP Daneway/Chalford*. Climb stile (and marvel at the superb view) and descend diagonally across field towards distant white house (Daneway Inn) and cross stile. Follow the path around the restored Daneway Portal, Sapperton Tunnel and enter Nature Reserve. The route follows a well trod path beside the course of the derelict Thames & Severn Canal, to the Daneway Inn.

SAPPERTON CANAL

TUNNEL (DISUSED)

Sapperton Park

© Goldeneye

Saltridge Wood

This could be described as a pub crawl, for the walk passes close to three popular inns, all with a reputation for good food. However, it also joins two delightful Cotswold villages affording wonderful views across a Cotswold landscape. Especially delightful are the trees in Saltridge Wood and the wildlife and flowers in the Nature Reserve. Best in early summer and autumn.

Distance
6 miles/9km.

Minimum Time
3 hours

Grade/Level of Difficulty
Easy/Moderate

Terrain/Paths
Woodland tracks, mud.

Landscape
Woodland, rolling pastureland, limestone villages.

Dogs
Keep under control in villages and on farm track/ tarmac road. Lots of woodland where dogs can run free.

Public Toilets
None

Parking (P)
Buckholt Wood, Cranham.

Recommended Start/Finish
Cranham

Location
Cranham and Sheepscombe are just off the B4070 between Stroud and Birdlip.

Link to other walks in this Guide
Short, 15 minute link to the Painswick-Slad Valley Walk via driveway to Down Barn Farm.

Features of Interest...

Cranham. This village has a mixed bag of architectural styles. It is not noted for its great aesthetics but divided by the Common and surrounded by beautiful woodlands to the north and south. Pretty church, popular pub and Cranham Feast in August.

Cranham Woods. Nature Reserve with a tangled web of pathways. The approach from Birdlip in early summer with the new foliage is memorable.

Saltridge Wood. Nature Reserve with paths that afford superb views down the valley towards Painswick.

Sheepscombe. A straggling village surrounded by beautiful woodland, rolling pastures and green hills. The view down the valley looking towards Painswick church is a beauty. It is the ancestral home of Laurie Lee whose parents moved to Slad. He maintained a connection with the village by purchasing the field for the cricket club, so named Laurie Field and which remains part of his Estate. A network of footpaths leads through woodland to Painswick, Cranham and Slad..

Where to Eat & Drink...

The Black Horse Inn, Cranham. Popular with local residents and walkers due to its proximity to the Cotswold Way. Homely and traditional bar serving food. Best to arrive early especially for Sunday lunch. 01452 812217

Butcher's Arms, Sheepscombe. The Butcher's Arms has an unlikely national claim to fame - the much photographed carved sign of a butcher sipping a pint of beer with a pig tethered to his leg. 'Pie and a Pint' meal deal. 01452 812113 www.butchers-arms.co.uk

Fostons Ash Inn, Slad Road. Situated on the B4070, this is a good meeting place and close to the mid-way point of this walk. This Grade II Cotswold stone inn is named after a former turnpike keeper and provides a comfortable venue for a meal or quick drink whatever the weather. Inside there are open log fires, areas for children and water bowls for the dog. Outside there is a terrace and garden for summer alfresco dining. 01452 863262

Far End

Far End Wood

Butcher's Arms

Lady's Wood

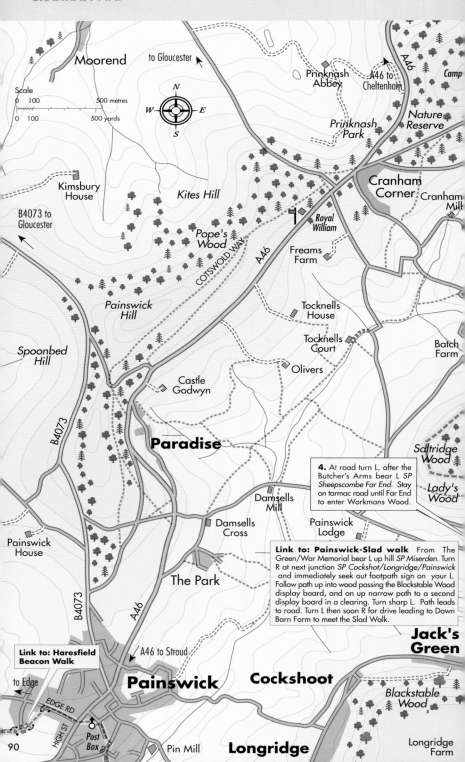

Moorend

to Gloucester

Scale
0   100   500 metres
0   100   500 yards

N
W — E
S

Prinknash
Abbey

A46 to
Cheltenham

A46

Camp

Prinknash
Park

Nature
Reserve

Kimsbury
House

Kites Hill

Cranham
Corner

Cranham
Mill

B4073 to
Gloucester

Pope's
Wood

COTSWOLD WAY

A46

Royal
William

Freams
Farm

Painswick
Hill

Tocknells
House

Tocknells
Court

Batch
Farm

Spoonbed
Hill

Castle
Godwyn

Olivers

Paradise

Saltridge
Wood

Lady's
Wood

B4073

Damsells
Mill

4. At road turn L, after the
Butcher's Arms bear L *SP
Sheepscombe Far End.* Stay
on tarmac road until Far End
to enter Workmans Wood.

Painswick
House

Damsells
Cross

Painswick
Lodge

Link to: Painswick-Slad walk From The
Green/War Memorial bear L up hill *SP Miserden.* Turn
R at next junction *SP Cockshot/Longridge/Painswick*
and immediately seek out footpath sign on your L.
Follow path up into wood passing the Blackstable Wood
display board, and on up narrow path to a second
display board in a clearing. Turn sharp L. Path leads
to road. Turn L then soon R for drive leading to Down
Barn Farm to meet the Slad Walk.

The Park

B4073

A46

**Jack's
Green**

**Link to: Haresfield
Beacon Walk**

to Edge

A46 to Stroud

EDGE RD

HIGH ST

Painswick

Cockshoot

Blackstable
Wood

Post
Box

Pin Mill

Longridge

Longridge
Farm

90

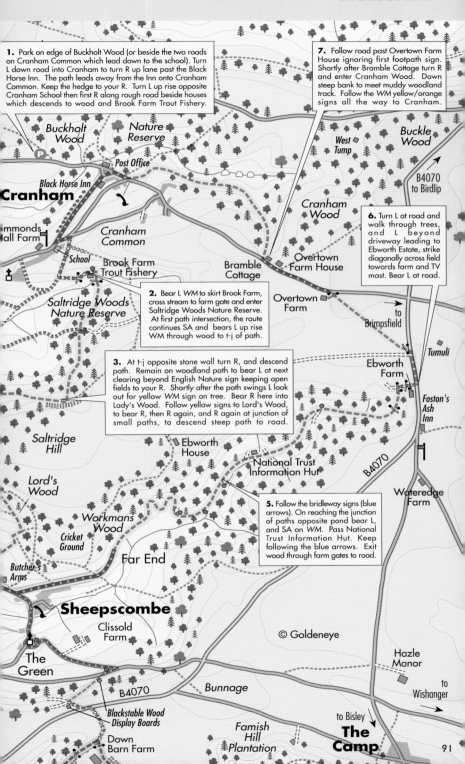

1. Park on edge of Buckholt Wood (or beside the two roads on Cranham Common which lead down to the school). Turn L down road into Cranham to turn R up lane past the Black Horse Inn. The path leads away from the Inn onto Cranham Common. Keep the hedge to your R. Turn L up rise opposite Cranham School then first R along rough road beside houses which descends to wood and Brook Farm Trout Fishery.

7. Follow road past Overtown Farm House ignoring first footpath sign. Shortly after Bramble Cottage turn R and enter Cranham Wood. Down steep bank to meet muddy woodland track. Follow the WM yellow/orange signs all the way to Cranham.

6. Turn L at road and walk through trees, and L beyond driveway leading to Ebworth Estate, strike diagonally across field towards farm and TV mast. Bear L at road.

2. Bear L WM to skirt Brook Farm, cross stream to farm gate and enter Saltridge Woods Nature Reserve. At first path intersection, the route continues SA and bears L up rise WM through wood to t-j of path.

3. At t-j opposite stone wall turn R, and descend path. Remain on woodland path to bear L at next clearing beyond English Nature sign keeping open fields to your R. Shortly after the path swings L look out for yellow WM sign on tree. Bear R here into Lady's Wood. Follow yellow signs to Lord's Wood, to bear R, then R again, and R again at junction of small paths, to descend steep path to road.

5. Follow the bridleway signs (blue arrows). On reaching the junction of paths opposite pond bear L, and SA on WM. Pass National Trust Information Hut. Keep following the blue arrows. Exit wood through farm gates to road.

Buckholt Wood

Nature Reserve

Post Office

Black Horse Inn

Cranham

immonds all Farm

School

Cranham Common

Brook Farm Trout Fishery

Saltridge Woods Nature Reserve

Saltridge Hill

Lord's Wood

Workmans Wood

Cricket Ground

Butcher's Arms

Sheepscombe

Clissold Farm

The Green

B4070

Blackstable Wood Display Boards

Down Barn Farm

Far End

Ebworth House

National Trust Information Hut

Bramble Cottage

Overtown Farm House

Overtown Farm

to Brimpsfield

Cranham Wood

West Tump

Buckle Wood

B4070 to Birdlip

Tumuli

Ebworth Farm

Foston's Ash Inn

B4070

Wateredge Farm

© Goldeneye

Hazle Manor

Bunnage

to Wishanger

to Bisley

Famish Hill Plantation

The Camp

91

View from beside the Woolpack Inn towards Furners Farm

This is the most strenuous of the walks in this book, and yet is perhaps the most rewarding. Certainly, you will have earned your pint in the Woolpack! The route takes you up and down Cotswold combes and provides breathtaking views of a very English landscape that so inspired the local boy, Laurie Lee, author of the classic 'Cider with Rosie'.

Distance
7.5 miles/11km.

Minimum Time
4.5 hours

Grade/Level of Difficulty
Moderate/Strenuous

Terrain/Paths
Mud, tracks, grass.

Landscape
Woodland, undulating pastureland.

Dogs
Keep under control around livestock. Lots of woodland where dogs can run free but will be on and off the lead a lot.

Public Toilets
Painswick

Parking (P)
Painswick or Bulls Cross.

Recommended Start/Finish
Painswick or Bulls Cross.

Location
Painswick lies between Stroud and Cheltenham on the A46. Slad is situated on the B4070 between Stroud and Birdlip.

Link to other walks in this Guide
To Haresfield Beacon or Cranham to Sheepscombe Walk via the Cotswold Way.

Features of Interest...

Catswood. Lovely woodland paths provide superb views across the valley.

Dillay Valley. A hidden Cotswold combe with magical qualities.

Laurie Lee. Poet, musician and traveller who was brought up in this valley, and who spent half his time here (the rest in Chelsea). His most famous book 'Cider with Rosie' captures an England long forgotten. If you have recently read it, you will recognise the valleys and woods.

Painswick. Its local description as 'The Queen of the Cotswolds' is fully justified. The houses and cottages are built from a grey, almost white limestone, in marked contrast to Broadway and Chipping Campden, and some of the buildings have an almost Palladian, yet statuesque quality about them. Look out for the Court House and the Cotswolds88hotel. Wander down the pretty side streets and visit the churchyard famous for the legendary 99 yew trees. The 100th yew tree has been planted time and again but has never survived. Painswick is one of the gems of the southern Cotswolds and is a worthy base from which to explore this region. It is also connected to a network of footpaths including the Cotswold Way so you can arrive by car or taxi and then just walk for the rest of your stay.

Rococo Garden. A beautiful C18 Rococo garden in 6 acres dating from a period of flamboyant and romantic garden design nestles in a hidden Cotswold valley. Be sure you visit in February for the display of magical snowdrops. Open daily mid-Jan to end Oct, 11-5. Restaurant and Gift Shop. 01452 813204 www.rococogarden.co.uk

Slad. One of the Stroud villages where cloth was spun in the little cottages before it all moved to South Riding, Yorkshire. Hundreds flock here to walk in the shadow of Laurie Lee's Cider With Rosie and to sample the brew still available in the Woolpack. You may wish to make your way to Bulls Cross, the hanging place, and now the start point for many walks. Laurie Lee lies buried in the churchyard, opposite the Woolpack. Surrounded by green pastures and ancient woodland.

St Mary's Church, Painswick. It is the soaring spire that will first captivate you then, as you enter, it will be the line of yew trees and then, as you wander around the churchyard, the tombs or monuments carved with their intricate figures. But do look up and admire the gold clock. The spire has been struck by lightning on many occasions including 1763 and 1883. The 100th yew tree always withers away.

Where to Eat & Drink...

JK's at St Michaels Restaurant, Victoria Street. This enthusiastically run restaurant with rooms has a weekly-changing menu. Everything is sourced locally, even berries and wild mushrooms in season from the nearby fields and hedgerows. B&B. 01452 813832 www.stmickshouse.com

Woolpack Inn, Slad. Traditional Cotswold pub with exceptional food, simply cooked, and home to a cup of Rosie's cider and the spirit of Laurie Lee. Newspaper, views, cricketers... A good halfway stopping point on the walk. 01452 813429 www.thewoolpackinn-slad.com

Where to Stay in Painswick...

Cotswolds88Hotel, Kemps Lane. This Palladian-style Cotswold rectory has been transformed by interior designer Marchella De Angelis into a lifestyle-boutique hotel in homage to the avant-garde artist, Leigh Bowery. 01452 813688 www.cotswolds88hotel.co.uk

St Anne's B&B, Gloucester Street. A listed C18 former wool merchant's house with a relaxed family atmosphere. Within easy walking distance of pubs and restaurants. 01452 812879 www.st-annes-painswick.co.uk

Cardynham House, Tibbiwell Street. A luxurious B&B set within an enchanting C15-16 former wool merchant's home. Each room is individually decorated from 'Old Tuscany' to 'Cottage Rose' but if you seek a real treat try the 'Pool Room'. Bistro. 01452 814006 www.cardynham.co.uk

Tibbiwell Lodge, Tibbiwell Lane. Perched on the valley side, Tibbiwell Lodge has good views and ample parking but is still just a short walk welcome. Dogs by arrangement. 01452 812748 www.tibbiwelllodgepainswick.webs.com

Troy House, Gloucester Street. A detached cottage with a pretty courtyard garden houses the B&B accommodation. Breakfast al fresco in fine weather. Children and dogs welcome. 01452 812339 www.troy-house.co.uk

St Mary's Church, Painswick

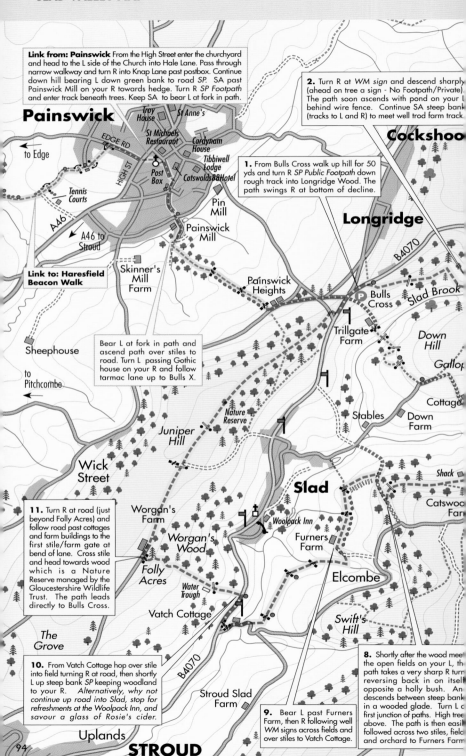

Link from: Painswick From the High Street enter the churchyard and head to the L side of the Church into Hale Lane. Pass through narrow walkway and turn R into Knap Lane past postbox. Continue down hill bearing L down green bank to road *SP*. SA past Painswick Mill on your R towards hedge. Turn R *SP Footpath* and enter track beneath trees. Keep SA to bear L at fork in path.

2. Turn R at *WM sign* and descend sharply (ahead on tree a sign - No Footpath/Private). The path soon ascends with pond on your L behind wire fence. Continue SA steep bank (tracks to L and R) to meet well trod farm track.

Painswick

Troy House
St Anne's
St Michaels Restaurant
EDGE RD
to Edge
Cardynam House
Tibbiwell Lodge
Cotswolds88Hotel
HIGH ST
Post Box
Pin Mill

A46
A46 to Stroud
Painswick Mill

Cockshoo

1. From Bulls Cross walk up hill for 50 yds and turn R *SP Public Footpath* down rough track into Longridge Wood. The path swings R at bottom of decline.

Longridge

B4070

Tennis Courts

Link to: Haresfield Beacon Walk

Skinner's Mill Farm

Painswick Heights

Bulls Cross
P

Slad Brook

Sheephouse

to Pitchcombe

Bear L at fork in path and ascend path over stiles to road. Turn L passing Gothic house on your R and follow tarmac lane up to Bulls X.

Trillgate Farm

Down Hill
Gallop

Nature Reserve

Juniper Hill

Stables

Down Farm

Cottage

Wick Street

Slad

Shack

Catswoo Far

11. Turn R at road (just beyond Folly Acres) and follow road past cottages and farm buildings to the first stile/farm gate at bend of lane. Cross stile and head towards wood which is a Nature Reserve managed by the Gloucestershire Wildlife Trust. The path leads directly to Bulls Cross.

Worgan's Farm

Woolpack Inn

Furners Farm

Worgan's Wood

Folly Acres

Water Trough

Vatch Cottage

Elcombe

Swift's Hill

The Grove

B4070

10. From Vatch Cottage hop over stile into field turning R at road, then shortly L up steep bank *SP* keeping woodland to your R. *Alternatively, why not continue up road into Slad, stop for refreshments at the Woolpack Inn, and savour a glass of Rosie's cider.*

Uplands

Stroud Slad Farm

9. Bear L past Furners Farm, then R following well WM signs across fields and over stiles to Vatch Cottage.

8. Shortly after the wood mee the open fields on your L, th path takes a very sharp R turn reversing back in on itsel opposite a holly bush. An descends between steep bank in a wooded glade. Turn L o first junction of paths. High tree above. The path is then easil followed across two stiles, fiel and orchard to Furners Farm

STROUD

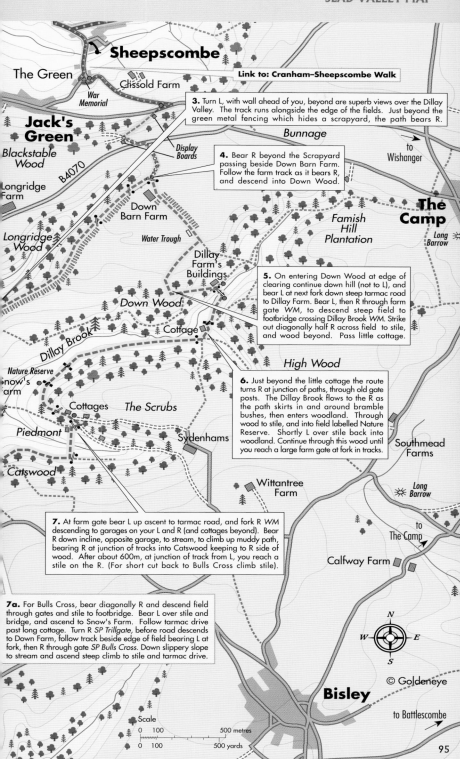

Sheepscombe

The Green

Clissold Farm

War Memorial

Link to: Cranham–Sheepscombe Walk

Jack's Green

Blackstable Wood

B4070

Longridge Farm

Longridge Wood

Display Boards

Down Barn Farm

Water Trough

Dillay Farm's Buildings

Down Wood

Dillay Brook

Cottage

Nature Reserve

Snow's Farm

Cottages

The Scrubs

Piedmont

Sydenhams

Catswood

Bunnage

to Wishanger

The Camp

Long Barrow

Famish Hill Plantation

High Wood

Southmead Farms

Long Barrow

Wittantree Farm

to The Camp

Calfway Farm

© Goldeneye

Bisley

to Battlescombe

3. Turn L, with wall ahead of you, beyond are superb views over the Dillay Valley. The track runs alongside the edge of the fields. Just beyond the green metal fencing which hides a scrapyard, the path bears R.

4. Bear R beyond the Scrapyard passing beside Down Barn Farm. Follow the farm track as it bears R, and descend into Down Wood.

5. On entering Down Wood at edge of clearing continue down hill (not to L), and bear L at next fork down steep tarmac road to Dillay Farm. Bear L, then R through farm gate *WM*, to descend steep field to footbridge crossing Dillay Brook *WM*. Strike out diagonally half R across field to stile, and wood beyond. Pass little cottage.

6. Just beyond the little cottage the route turns R at junction of paths, through old gate posts. The Dillay Brook flows to the R as the path skirts in and around bramble bushes, then enters woodland. Through wood to stile, and into field labelled Nature Reserve. Shortly L over stile back into woodland. Continue through this wood until you reach a large farm gate at fork in tracks.

7. At farm gate bear L up ascent to tarmac road, and fork R *WM* descending to garages on your L and R (and cottages beyond). Bear R down incline, opposite garage, to stream, to climb up muddy path, bearing R at junction of tracks into Catswood keeping to R side of wood. After about 600m, at junction of track from L, you reach a stile on the R. (For short cut back to Bulls Cross climb stile).

7a. For Bulls Cross, bear diagonally R and descend field through gates and stile to footbridge. Bear L over stile and bridge, and ascend to Snow's Farm. Follow tarmac drive past long cottage. Turn R *SP Trillgate*, before road descends to Down Farm, follow track beside edge of field bearing L at fork, then R through gate *SP Bulls Cross*. Down slippery slope to stream and ascend steep climb to stile and tarmac drive.

Scale

0   100   500 metres

0   100   500 yards

Haresfield Beacon

The route follows part of the Cotswold Way on the edge of the escarpment which affords spectacular views across the Vale of Gloucester, Severn Estuary and Wales. It then passes by an Iron Age fort and through some of Britain's most ancient woodland. The link to the Painswick-Slad walk allows for an interesting contrast.

Distance
5 miles/8km

Minimum Time
3 hours

Grade/Level of Difficulty
Easy/Moderate

Terrain/Paths
Mud, tracks and grass.

Landscape
Woodland, Cotswold escarpment and pastures.

Dogs
Some livestock and farms where dogs must be kept under control. Lots of woodland where they can run free.

Public Toilets
None

Parking (P)
Shortwood or Haresfield Beacon.

Recommended Start/Finish
Shortwood Car Park.

Location
East of Stroud with access via the B4008, off the A419.

Link to other walks in this Guide
To Painswick to Slad Valley Walk via the Cotswold Way.

Features of Interest...

Cromwell's Stone. Laid here to celebrate the Parliamentarians successful siege of Gloucester in 1643.

Edge. As its name suggests, a group of cottages overlook the Painswick Valley, on the edge of the escarpment. Pretty village green.

Haresfield Beacon. High open grassland at 700 feet that was a natural fort for Iron Age and Roman settlements. Provides panoramic views of the Severn Estuary, Forest of Dean and Vale of Gloucester.

Shortwood Topograph. Displays the visible landscape in relief and illustrates views.

Standish Wood. An area of ancient woodland recorded in 1297. The wood is delightful when the bluebells and primroses bloom in Spring.

Where to Eat & Drink...

Edgemoor Inn, Edge. The late C19 Inn is well known for its pretty panoramic views and has an extensive terrace overlooking Painswick & surrounding countryside. Good selection of food. 01452 813576 www.edgemoor-inn.com

Where to Stay...

Upper Doreys Mill, Edge. A C18 stone Mill House set in a beautiful garden complete with stream. Guest lounge with log fire. No dogs. 01452 812459 www.doreys.co.uk

Cromwell's Stone

Standish Wood

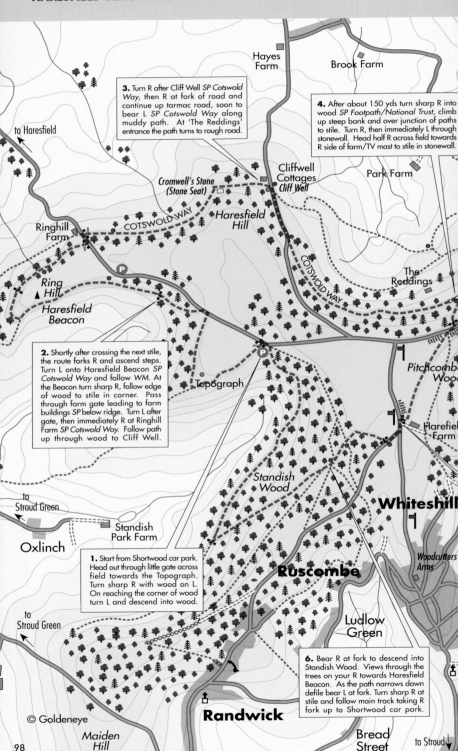

3. Turn R after Cliff Well *SP Cotswold Way*, then R at fork of road and continue up tarmac road, soon to bear L *SP Cotswold Way* along muddy path. At 'The Reddings' entrance the path turns to rough road.

4. After about 150 yds turn sharp R into wood *SP Footpath/National Trust*, climb up steep bank and over junction of paths to stile. Turn R, then immediately L through stonewall. Head half R across field towards R side of farm/TV mast to stile in stonewall.

2. Shortly after crossing the next stile, the route forks R and ascend steps. Turn L onto Haresfield Beacon *SP Cotswold Way* and follow *WM*. At the Beacon turn sharp R, follow edge of wood to stile in corner. Pass through farm gate leading to farm buildings *SP* below ridge. Turn L after gate, then immediately R at Ringhill Farm *SP Cotswold Way*. Follow path up through wood to Cliff Well.

1. Start from Shortwood car park. Head out through little gate across field towards the Topograph. Turn sharp R with wood on L. On reaching the corner of wood turn L and descend into wood.

6. Bear R at fork to descend into Standish Wood. Views through the trees on your R towards Haresfield Beacon. As the path narrows down defile bear L at fork. Turn sharp R at stile and follow main track taking R fork up to Shortwood car park.

Hayes Farm

Brook Farm

to Haresfield

Cromwell's Stone (Stone Seat)

Cliffwell Cottages
Cliff Well

Park Farm

COTSWOLD WAY

Haresfield Hill

Ringhill Farm

Ring Hill

Haresfield Beacon

COTSWOLD WAY

The Reddings

Topograph

Pitchcomb Woo

Harefie Farm

to Stroud Green

Standish Park Farm

Standish Wood

Whiteshill

Oxlinch

to Stroud Green

Ruscombe

Woodcutters Arms

Ludlow Green

© Goldeneye

Randwick

Maiden Hill

Bread Street

to Stroud

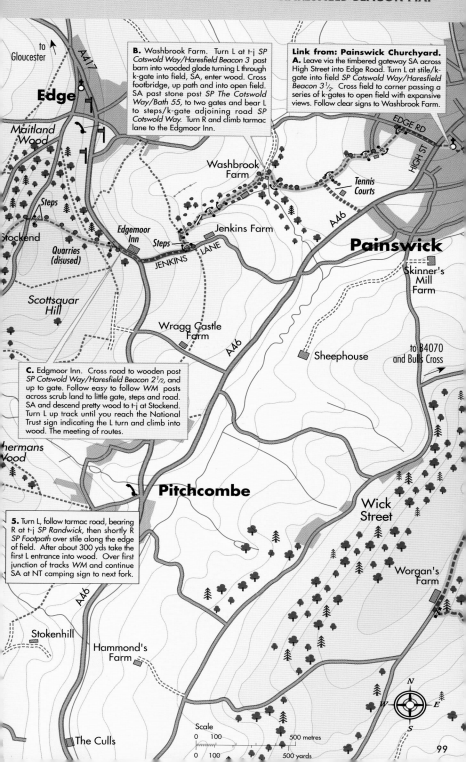

B. Washbrook Farm. Turn L at t-j SP *Cotswold Way/Haresfield Beacon 3* past barn into wooded glade turning L through k-gate into field, SA, enter wood. Cross footbridge, up path and into open field. SA past stone post *SP The Cotswold Way/Bath 55*, to two gates and bear L to steps/k-gate adjoining road *SP Cotswold Way.* Turn R and climb tarmac lane to the Edgemoor Inn.

Link from: Painswick Churchyard.
A. Leave via the timbered gateway SA across High Street into Edge Road. Turn L at stile/k-gate into field *SP Cotswold Way/Haresfield Beacon 3½.* Cross field to corner passing a series of k-gates to open field with expansive views. Follow clear signs to Washbrook Farm.

to Gloucester

A417

Edge

Maitland Wood

Washbrook Farm

EDGE RD

HIGH ST

Tennis Courts

Painswick

A46

Steps

Stockend

Edgemoor Inn

Steps

Jenkins Farm

JENKINS LANE

Skinner's Mill Farm

Quarries (disused)

Scottsquar Hill

Wragg Castle Farm

A46

Sheephouse

to B4070 and Bulls Cross

C. Edgemoor Inn. Cross road to wooden post *SP Cotswold Way/Haresfield Beacon 2½,* and up to gate. Follow easy to follow *WM* posts across scrub land to little gate, steps and road. SA and descend pretty wood to t-j at Stockend. Turn L up track until you reach the National Trust sign indicating the L turn and climb into wood. The meeting of routes.

hermans Wood

Pitchcombe

Wick Street

5. Turn L, follow tarmac road, bearing R at t-j *SP Randwick,* then shortly R *SP Footpath* over stile along the edge of field. After about 300 yds take the first L entrance into wood. Over first junction of tracks *WM* and continue SA at NT camping sign to next fork.

Worgan's Farm

A46

Stokenhill

Hammond's Farm

The Culls

N
W   E
S

Scale
0   100
0   100
500 metres
500 yards

View towards Downham Hill

The first walk around the ramparts of Uley Bury, the Iron Age hill fort is easy-going and pushchair-friendly for young families. The views are spectacular. Thereafter, the route across Cam Long Down, along the Cotswold Way is equally spectacular with fine views towards the River Severn and Welsh Hills. Be prepared for a couple of stiff climbs.

Distance
Walk 1: 1.25 miles/2km.
Walk 2: 4 miles/6.4km.

Minimum Time
Walk 1: 1 hour
Walk 2: 2.5 hours.

Grade/Level of Difficulty
Easy/Moderate

Terrain/Paths
Grass and farm tracks.

Landscape
Outcrops of limestone hillocks, and the escarpment. Patchwork of fields.

Dogs
Uley Bury walk is popular with local dog walkers as there is not much livestock. The longer walk has more livestock – dogs to be kept under control at all times.

Public Toilets
None

Parking (P)
Uley Bury

Recommended Start/Finish
Uley Bury P

Location
Uley is between Stroud and Dursley on the B4066.

Features of Interest...

Cam Long Down. A humpbacked ridge of oolitic limestone that once seen is never forgotten. From the top it's a good viewpoint touched by the Cotswold Way surrounded by beech woods and bracken.

Hetty Pegler's Tump (Uley Tumulus). Neolithic Long Barrow 120ft x 22ft, 4 chambers, 38 skeletons found in C19. Torch and Wellington boots needed.

St Giles' Church, Uley. In a spectacular position overlooking the valley. Noted for the Norman font, fine roof and stained glass.

Owlpen Manor. An iconic group of picturesque Cotswold buildings: Manor House, Tithe Barn, Church, Mill and Court House. Water Garden and terrace. The Tudor manor dates from 1450 to 1616 but the whole estate has 900 years of history to tell. Holiday cottages for hire. 01453 860261 www.owlpen.com

The Old Brewery, Uley. The mill owner, Samuel Price, built this brewery in 1833 to assuage his workers' thirst. It was restored in 1984 and has since won many awards for their Old Spot, Pigs Ear and Uley Bitter. It is not open to prying visitors, only the trade. You can sample their wares in the Old Crown Inn at the top of the village, or in various hostelries around the Cotswolds.

Uley. A long, attractive village with some fine Georgian houses. Famous centre of cloth in the C17 and C18. In 1608 three Uley clothiers represented 29 local weavers of broadcloth, and also, the 13 weavers from Owlpen. Roman settlement.

Uley Bury Iron Age Hill Fort. This is the Cotswolds' most famous Iron Age site. The deep ramparts provide superb views across the Severn Vale, Welsh Hills, Dursley and Owlpen Woods. An enclosed area of about 32 acres used for arable crops.

The Ramparts of Uley Bury

Cam Long Down

Where to Eat, Drink, Sleep...

Rowden House, 31 Elcombe Lane. Located just south of the map but still a useful billet for the Cotswold Way and touring the South Cotswolds. Two comfortable double rooms and a single, for a peaceful nights sleep and lovely country views. Dogs welcome. 01453 861134 www.rowdenbandb.co.uk

The Old Crown Inn, Uley. C17 Inn on village green. Lunch and evening meals as well as cream teas in the afternoons. Serves real ale from the local Uley brewery. B&B. 01453 860502 www.theoldcrownuley.co.uk

Where to Eat & Drink just off the map...

Rose & Crown Inn, Nympsfield. Good food served in restaurant and bar. B&B. Children and dogs welcome. 01453 860240

The Old Brewery, Uley

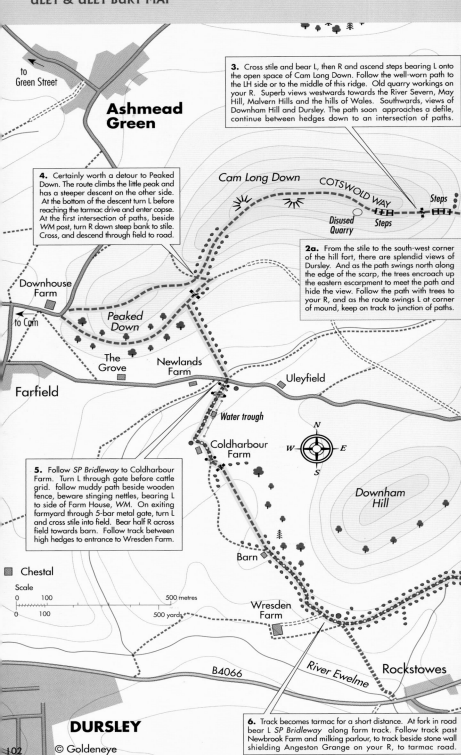

Ashmead Green

to Green Street

3. Cross stile and bear L, then R and ascend steps bearing L onto the open space of Cam Long Down. Follow the well-worn path to the LH side or to the middle of this ridge. Old quarry workings on your R. Superb views westwards towards the River Severn, May Hill, Malvern Hills and the hills of Wales. Southwards, views of Downham Hill and Dursley. The path soon approaches a defile, continue between hedges down to an intersection of paths.

Cam Long Down COTSWOLD WAY

Steps

Steps

Disused Quarry

4. Certainly worth a detour to Peaked Down. The route climbs the little peak and has a steeper descent on the other side. At the bottom of the descent turn L before reaching the tarmac drive and enter copse. At the first intersection of paths, beside *WM* post, turn R down steep bank to stile. Cross, and descend through field to road.

2a. From the stile to the south-west corner of the hill fort, there are splendid views of Dursley. And as the path swings north along the edge of the scarp, the trees encroach up the eastern escarpment to meet the path and hide the view. Follow the path with trees to your R, and as the route swings L at corner of mound, keep on track to junction of paths.

Downhouse Farm

to Cam

Peaked Down

The Grove

Newlands Farm

Uleyfield

Farfield

Water trough

5. Follow *SP Bridleway* to Coldharbour Farm. Turn L through gate before cattle grid. follow muddy path beside wooden fence, beware stinging nettles, bearing L to side of Farm House, *WM*. On exiting farmyard through 5-bar metal gate, turn L and cross stile into field. Bear half R across field towards barn. Follow track between high hedges to entrance to Wresden Farm.

Coldharbour Farm

N
W ● E
S

Downham Hill

Barn

Wresden Farm

■ Chestal

Scale
0 100   500 metres
0 100   500 yards

Rockstowes

B4066   *River Ewelme*

DURSLEY

© Goldeneye

6. Track becomes tarmac for a short distance. At fork in road bear L *SP Bridleway* along farm track. Follow track past Newbrook Farm and milking parlour, to track beside stone wall shielding Angeston Grange on your R, to tarmac road.

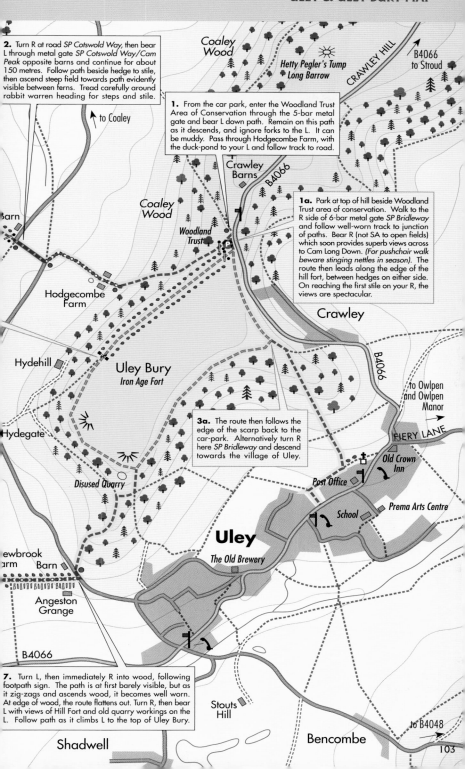

Coaley Wood

Hetty Pegler's Tump
Long Barrow

CRAWLEY HILL

B4066
to Stroud

2. Turn R at road *SP Cotswold Way,* then bear L through metal gate *SP Cotswold Way/Cam Peak* opposite barns and continue for about 150 metres. Follow path beside hedge to stile, then ascend steep field towards path evidently visible between ferns. Tread carefully around rabbit warren heading for steps and stile.

1. From the car park, enter the Woodland Trust Area of Conservation through the 5-bar metal gate and bear L down path. Remain on this path as it descends, and ignore forks to the L. It can be muddy. Pass through Hodgecombe Farm, with the duck-pond to your L and follow track to road.

↑ to Coaley

Crawley Barns

B4066

Coaley Wood

Woodland Trust

Barn

Hodgecombe Farm

1a. Park at top of hill beside Woodland Trust area of conservation. Walk to the R side of 6-bar metal gate *SP Bridleway* and follow well-worn track to junction of paths. Bear R (not SA to open fields) which soon provides superb views across to Cam Long Down. *(For pushchair walk beware stinging nettles in season).* The route then leads along the edge of the hill fort, between hedges on either side. On reaching the first stile on your R, the views are spectacular.

Crawley

Hydehill

Uley Bury
Iron Age Fort

B4066

to Owlpen and Owlpen Manor

Hydegate

FIERY LANE

3a. The route then follows the edge of the scarp back to the car-park. Alternatively turn R here *SP Bridleway* and descend towards the village of Uley.

Old Crown Inn

Post Office

Disused Quarry

School

Prema Arts Centre

Uley

ewbrook arm   Barn

The Old Brewery

Angeston Grange

B4066

7. Turn L, then immediately R into wood, following footpath sign. The path is at first barely visible, but as it zig-zags and ascends wood, it becomes well worn. At edge of wood, the route flattens out. Turn R, then bear L with views of Hill Fort and old quarry workings on the L. Follow path as it climbs L to the top of Uley Bury.

Stouts Hill

to B4048

Shadwell

Bencombe

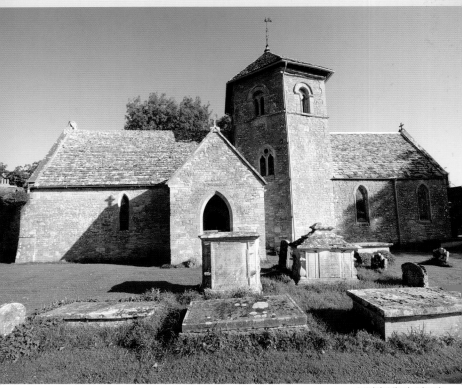

St Nicholas' Church, Ozleworth

Perhaps the remotest and most isolated of these walks. These deep combes are havens for wildlife and flowers, and are overlooked by sweeping sheep pastures. And yet, dotted along this remote area are gems of domestic architecture such as manor houses with their little churches. A picnic or supplies for the walk are recommended.

Distance
Walk 1: 1.5 miles/2.4km.
Walk 2: 5 miles/8km.

Minimum Time
Walk 1: 1 hour.
Walk 2: 2.5 hours.

Grade/Level of Difficulty
Easy

Terrain/Paths
Woodland tracks, grass.

Landscape
Valleys, pastures and woodland.

Dogs
Keep under control - beware livestock in farm fields.

Public Toilets
None

Parking (P)
Ozleworth

Recommended Start/Finish
Ozleworth

Location
Two miles east of Wotton-under-Edge. Best approached from the junction of the B4058 and A4135, Dursley-Tetbury road.

Features of Interest...

Boxwell Court. C15 origins, formerly owned by Gloucester Cathedral. Tudor doorway.

BT Tower.
Built in 1965. 240 ft high at 750 ft above sea level.

Lasborough Manor. Built in 1630 for Sir Thomas Estcourt. Renaissance chimney pots. Enormous bay windows of three storeys. Estcourt heraldry.

Lasborough Park. C18 monuments and stained glass. Tudor gothic style, castellated with four towers.

Newark Park, Ozleworth (NT). Former Tudor hunting lodge with an eclectic art collection. Countryside walks. Plant sales. Open Mar to May W & Th, (& W/Es June to 1 Nov) 11-5. 01793 817666 www.nationaltrust.org.uk

Ozleworth Bottom. Wild, remote and beautiful. A deep combe with wild flowers, birdlife and ancient woodlands. A thriving valley in the C17 and C18s when 15 fulling mills (to cleanse and thicken cloth) operated within 5 miles.

Ozleworth Park.
C18 house with spacious lawns. Rose Garden.

St Bartholomew's Church, Newington Bagpath. Private church boarded up. Jacobean pulpit. West tower and chancel rebuilt in 1858.

St Mary's Church, Lasborough. Norman font and elaborate roof trusses. Rebuilt 1861-62.

St Mary the Virgin's Church, Boxwell.
C13 origins. Massive stone bellcote and grotesque corbels.

St Nicholas' Church, Ozleworth. Extremely rare C12 hexagonal tower. Norman remains. Rare weathercock. C13 font and Clutterbuck monument.

Where to Eat & Drink just off the map...

Black Horse Inn, North Nibley. Family-run country inn with restaurant and public bar, live music nights and reported ghostly sightings! B&B. 01453 543777
www.blackhorsenorthnibley.co.uk

Royal Oak, Leighterton. Recent renovations of contemporary décor, coupled with locally-sourced produce and a child friendly ambience make up the ingredients for this popular dining pub. Large garden. 01666 890250
www.royaloakleighterton.co.uk

Where to Stay just off the map...

Calcot Manor. This is a leisure complex combining a country house hotel with spa. All the pampering you may well desire after a day in the combes and hills of Gloucestershire. Gumstool Inn is next door for a glass of ale and pub grub. 01666 890391
www.calcotmanor.co.uk

North Nibley House. This grade II listed C17 manor house lying on the Cotswold Way is a working farm set in 2.5 acres of flower-filled gardens, and 200 acres of farmland, and woods. If you seek a unique B&B experience in old-fashioned style, try it. Guests have their own sitting/dining room. Small campsite. 01453 543108
www.nibleyhouse.co.uk

Newington Bagpath

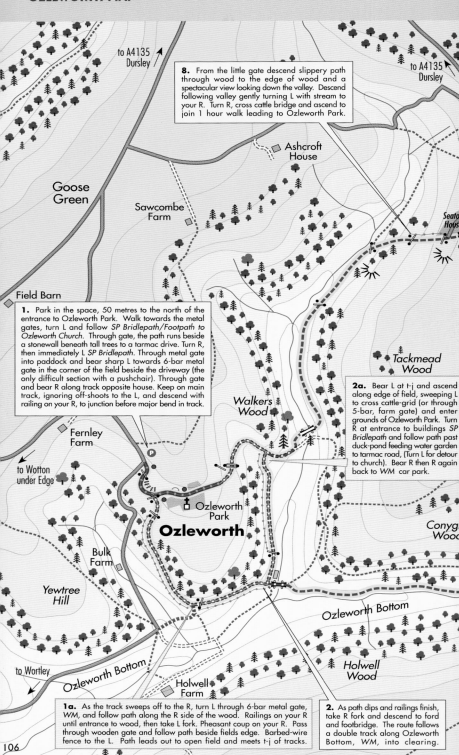

to A4135 Dursley

to A4135 Dursley

8. From the little gate descend slippery path through wood to the edge of wood and a spectacular view looking down the valley. Descend following valley gently turning L with stream to your R. Turn R, cross cattle bridge and ascend to join 1 hour walk leading to Ozleworth Park.

Ashcroft House

Goose Green

Sawcombe Farm

Seator House

Field Barn

1. Park in the space, 50 metres to the north of the entrance to Ozleworth Park. Walk towards the metal gates, turn L and follow *SP Bridlepath/Footpath to Ozleworth Church*. Through gate, the path runs beside a stonewall beneath tall trees to a tarmac drive. Turn R, then immediately L *SP Bridlepath*. Through metal gate into paddock and bear sharp L towards 6-bar metal gate in the corner of the field beside the driveway (the only difficult section with a pushchair). Through gate and bear R along track opposite house. Keep on main track, ignoring off-shoots to the L, and descend with railing on your R, to junction before major bend in track.

Tackmead Wood

2a. Bear L at t-j and ascend along edge of field, sweeping L to cross cattle-grid (or through 5-bar, farm gate) and enter grounds of Ozleworth Park. Turn R at entrance to buildings *SP Bridlepath* and follow path past duck-pond feeding water garden to tarmac road, (Turn L for detour to church). Bear R then R again back to *WM* car park.

Walkers Wood

Fernley Farm

to Wotton under Edge

Ozleworth Park

Ozleworth

Conygr Wood

Bulk Farm

Yewtree Hill

Ozleworth Bottom

Ozleworth Bottom

to Wortley

Holwell Farm

Holwell Wood

1a. As the track sweeps off to the R, turn L through 6-bar metal gate, *WM*, and follow path along the R side of the wood. Railings on your R until entrance to wood, then take L fork. Pheasant coup on your R. Pass through wooden gate and follow path beside fields edge. Barbed-wire fence to the L. Path leads out to open field and meets t-j of tracks.

2. As path dips and railings finish, take R fork and descend to ford and footbridge. The route follows a double track along Ozleworth Bottom, *WM*, into clearing.

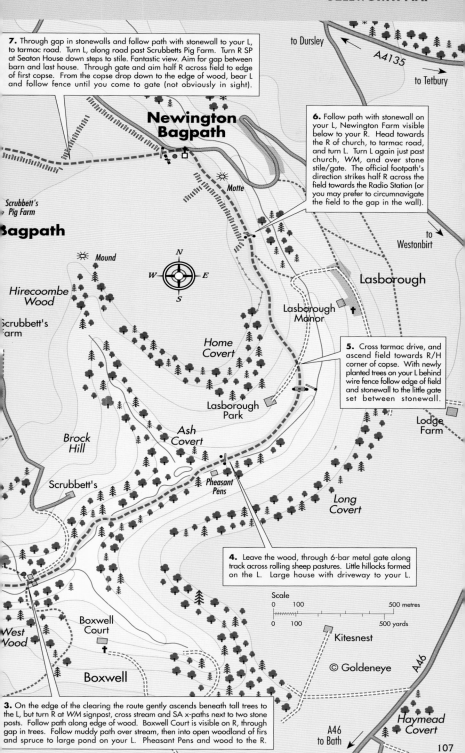

7. Through gap in stonewalls and follow path with stonewall to your L, to tarmac road. Turn L, along road past Scrubbetts Pig Farm. Turn R SP at Seaton House down steps to stile. Fantastic view. Aim for gap between barn and last house. Through gate and aim half R across field to edge of first copse. From the copse drop down to the edge of wood, bear L and follow fence until you come to gate (not obviously in sight).

to Dursley

to Tetbury

A4135

Newington Bagpath

6. Follow path with stonewall on your L, Newington Farm visible below to your R. Head towards the R of church, to tarmac road, and turn L. Turn L again just past church, WM, and over stone stile/gate. The official footpath's direction strikes half R across the field towards the Radio Station (or you may prefer to circumnavigate the field to the gap in the wall).

Motte

Scrubbett's Pig Farm

Bagpath

☼ Mound

Hirecoombe Wood

Scrubbett's Farm

N
W E
S

to Westonbirt

Lasborough

Lasborough Manor ✝

Home Covert

5. Cross tarmac drive, and ascend field towards R/H corner of copse. With newly planted trees on your L behind wire fence follow edge of field and stonewall to the little gate set between stonewall.

Lasborough Park

Brock Hill

Ash Covert

Lodge Farm

Scrubbett's

Pheasant Pens

Long Covert

4. Leave the wood, through 6-bar metal gate along track across rolling sheep pastures. Little hillocks formed on the L. Large house with driveway to your L.

Scale
0   100   500 metres
0   100   500 yards

West Wood

Boxwell Court ✝

Kitesnest

© Goldeneye

A46

Boxwell

Haymead Covert

A46
to Bath

3. On the edge of the clearing the route gently ascends beneath tall trees to the L, but turn R at WM signpost, cross stream and SA x-paths next to two stone posts. Follow path along edge of wood. Boxwell Court is visible on R, through gap in trees. Follow muddy path over stream, then into open woodland of firs and spruce to large pond on your L. Pheasant Pens and wood to the R.

Overlooking Lower Colham and the By Brook Valley

Here you have one of England's prettiest villages hidden away in a deep wooded combe. Take in the lovely old world cottages and follow the path idly through the woods, with the shimmering By Brook below. The walk incorporates a section of the Colham Farm Trail, a circular trail that takes you through ancient woodland in Parsonage Wood and down into the By Brook valley where the meadow is a Site of Special Scientific Interest. Resident species include the green winged meadow orchid.

Distance
Walk 1: 2.75 miles/4.4km.
Walk 2: 5.25 miles/8.4km.

Minimum Time
Walk 1: 2.5 hours.
Walk 2: 1 hour.

Grade/Level of Difficulty
Easy

Terrain/Paths
Woodland tracks, grass.

Landscape
Wooded combe

Dogs
Well trod path with few stiles - fairly good for dogs.

Public Toilets
Below the bridge at Castle Combe.

Parking (P)
Car park at the top of Castle Combe.

Recommended Start/Finish
Opposite the Dower House in Castle Combe

Location
Castle Combe is situated midway between Chippenham and Chipping Sodbury. It is best approached from Chippenham via the A420 (Chippenham to Bristol), and from the north from the A46 (Stroud to Bath) via the villages of Badminton/Acton Turville.

Features of Interest...

Castle Combe. One of the prettiest and most visited villages in the Cotswolds lies sheltered in a hidden valley surrounded by steep, wooded hills. It takes its name from the Norman castle on the hilltop above. In former times, it was an important medieval wool centre as evidenced by the weavers and clothiers' cottages that descend from the Market Cross to By Brook, and the three-arch bridge. Nowadays, the popularity of the village as a tourist destination means there are gift shops and inns. Its great claim to fame followed its appearance in the 1966 film of Doctor Doolittle starring Rex Harrison. The village remains a popular location for TV commercials and period dramas because of its rows of quaint cottages undisturbed by time. www.castle-combe.com

Dower House. The finest house in the village built in the C17. Note the beautiful shell-hooded doorway.

Long Dean. A cluster of small cottages that were probably built for workers of the disused mill now a spacious home.

Ford. Village on the busy A420, but a welcome stop if you've developed a hunger and a thirst.

Motor Racing Circuit. Regular car and motorcycle race days take place through the summer at this circuit, one of the longest established race tracks in the UK. 01249 782417 www.castlecombecircuit.co.uk

St Andrew's Church, Castle Combe. Originally C13, the nave was added in the C14 and the tower completed in the C16. In the 1850s much of the church had to be rebuilt. Note the beautiful fan vaulting reminiscent of Bath Abbey. Also the medieval faceless clock, one of the most ancient working clocks in the country.

Village Museum. Run by villagers, this tiny museum gives a fascinating insight into the history of the village and its surrounding countryside. Many artefacts including archaeological finds and old photographs and maps. Open East to Oct Su and BHs 2-5 or by prior arrangement. 01249 782250 www.museum.castle-combe.com

Descent into Long Dean

Castle Combe

Where to Eat & Drink...

Castle Inn Hotel. This is a pretty honey-coloured building set in the market place. Many features of the original C12 construction remain thanks to subtle restoration. The eleven bedrooms are individual in character. You can choose fine dining in the restaurant or more simple bar food in the bar itself. Elegant dining in a very pleasant setting. 01249 783030 www.castle-inn.info

White Hart, Market Place. C14 pub at the heart of the village with a sunny conservatory and patio gardens to the rear. 01249 782295

White Hart Inn, Ford. A rambling C16 coaching inn situated in the Wyvern Valley beside a trout stream and with a large beer garden. B&B. Children welcome. 01249 782213

Where to Stay...

Fosse Farmhouse B&B. Set conveniently close to the north-west corner of this walk. Caron's home is beautifully furnished in English Vintage and French Brocante. You will be made very welcome, and your hostess is a source of abundant information. Dogs and children welcomed. Self-catering. 01249 782286 www.fossefarmhouse.com

Georgian House B&B. Ideally situated in the village centre next to the White Hart Pub and opposite the Castle Inn. The house's exterior was used as Hercule Poirot's home in The Murder of Roger Ackroyd. One bedroom of simple and comfortable design. Your hostess, Lady Margaret, is a devotee and authority on Greek Orthodoxy. 01249 783009

Manor House Hotel. More Surrey country club than Cotswold Manor, and with its fine golf course is probably not geared for walkers. However, it shadows the village lying hidden away in 365 acres of gardens and woodland. You can stay in the Mews Cottages, too, if you prefer. 01249 782206 www.manorhouse.co.uk

Where to Stay just off the map...

White House B&B, Nettleton. Set in open countryside two miles outside Castle Combe. Accommodation is in an annexe to a thatched cottage containing bedroom and shower room. There are plenty of places to sit and relax in the orchard and garden. 01249 782359 www.thewhitehousebandb.com

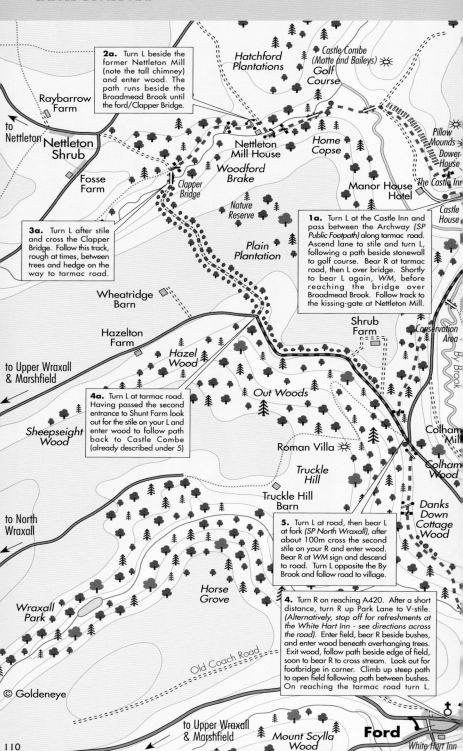

2a. Turn L beside the former Nettleton Mill (note the tall chimney) and enter wood. The path runs beside the Broadmead Brook until the ford/Clapper Bridge.

Hatchford Plantations

Castle Combe (Motte and Baileys) ☀

Golf Course

to Nettleton

Raybarrow Farm

Nettleton Shrub

Nettleton Mill House

Home Copse

Pillow Mounds

Dower House

Fosse Farm

Clapper Bridge

Woodford Brake

Manor House Hotel

The Castle Inn

Castle House

Nature Reserve

1a. Turn L at the Castle Inn and pass between the Archway (SP Public Footpath) along tarmac road. Ascend lane to stile and turn L, following a path beside stonewall to golf course. Bear R at tarmac road, then L over bridge. Shortly to bear L again, WM, before reaching the bridge over Broadmead Brook. Follow track to the kissing-gate at Nettleton Mill.

3a. Turn L after stile and cross the Clapper Bridge. Follow this track, rough at times, between trees and hedge on the way to tarmac road.

Plain Plantation

Shrub Farm

Conservation Area

Wheatridge Barn

Hazelton Farm

Hazel Wood

By Brook

to Upper Wraxall & Marshfield

Out Woods

4a. Turn L at tarmac road. Having passed the second entrance to Shunt Farm look out for the stile on your L and enter wood to follow path back to Castle Combe (already described under 5)

Sheepseight Wood

Roman Villa ☀

Colham Mill

Colham Wood

Truckle Hill

to North Wraxall

Truckle Hill Barn

Danks Down Cottage Wood

5. Turn L at road, then bear L at fork (SP North Wraxall), after about 100m cross the second stile on your R and enter wood. Bear R at WM sign and descend to road. Turn L opposite the By Brook and follow road to village.

Horse Grove

Wraxall Park

4. Turn R on reaching A420. After a short distance, turn R up Park Lane to V-stile. (Alternatively, stop off for refreshments at the White Hart Inn - see directions across the road). Enter field, bear R beside bushes, and enter wood beneath overhanging trees. Exit wood, follow path beside edge of field, soon to bear R to cross stream. Look out for footbridge in corner. Climb up steep path to open field following path between bushes. On reaching the tarmac road turn L.

Old Coach Road

© Goldeneye

to Upper Wraxall & Marshfield

Mount Scylla Wood

Ford

White Hart Inn

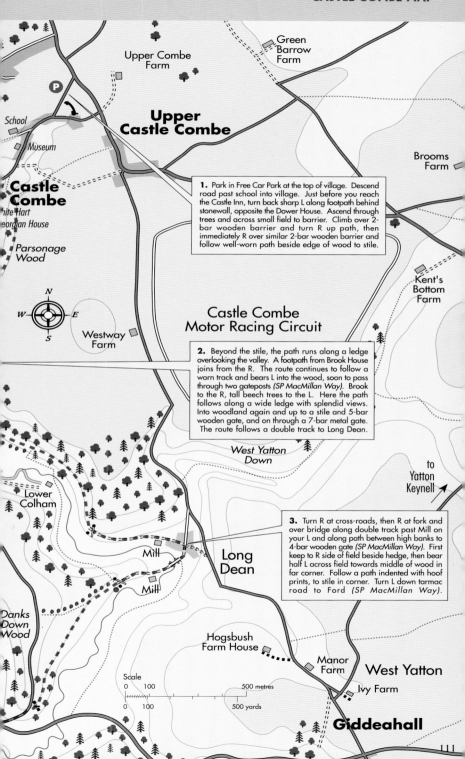

Green
Barrow
Farm

Upper Combe
Farm

P

**Upper
Castle Combe**

School

Museum

Brooms
Farm

**Castle
Combe**

White Hart
Georgian House

Parsonage
Wood

Kent's
Bottom
Farm

1. Park in Free Car Park at the top of village. Descend road past school into village. Just before you reach the Castle Inn, turn back sharp L along footpath behind stonewall, opposite the Dower House. Ascend through trees and across small field to barrier. Climb over 2-bar wooden barrier and turn R up path, then immediately R over similar 2-bar wooden barrier and follow well-worn path beside edge of wood to stile.

N
W · E
S

Westway
Farm

**Castle Combe
Motor Racing Circuit**

2. Beyond the stile, the path runs along a ledge overlooking the valley. A footpath from Brook House joins from the R. The route continues to follow a worn track and bears L into the wood, soon to pass through two gateposts *(SP MacMillan Way)*. Brook to the R, tall beech trees to the L. Here the path follows along a wide ledge with splendid views. Into woodland again and up to a stile and 5-bar wooden gate, and on through a 7-bar metal gate. The route follows a double track to Long Dean.

*West Yatton
Down*

to
Yatton
Keynell

Lower
Colham

Mill

**Long
Dean**

Mill

3. Turn R at cross-roads, then R at fork and over bridge along double track past Mill on your L and along path between high banks to 4-bar wooden gate *(SP MacMillan Way)*. First keep to R side of field beside hedge, then bear half L across field towards middle of wood in far corner. Follow a path indented with hoof prints, to stile in corner. Turn L down tarmac road to Ford *(SP MacMillan Way)*.

Danks
Down
Wood

Hogsbush
Farm House

Manor
Farm

West Yatton

Ivy Farm

Scale
0   100   500 metres
0   100   500 yards

Giddeahall

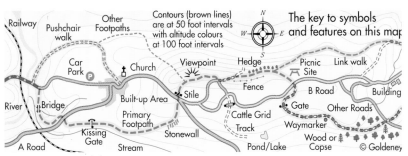

Railway

Pushchair walk

Other Footpaths

Contours (brown lines) are at 50 foot intervals with altitude colours at 100 foot intervals

The key to symbols and features on this map

Car Park

Church

Viewpoint

Hedge

Picnic Site

Link walk

Built-up Area

Stile

Fence

B Road

Building

River

Bridge

Primary Footpath

Cattle Grid

Gate

Other Roads

Kissing Gate

Stonewall

Track

Waymarker

A Road

Stream

Pond/Lake

Wood or Copse

© Goldeney